Praise for NURTURE

"Lisa Bevere has revelation from the heart of God for His daughters! NURTURE will position women of all ages for purpose and destiny while bringing healing and restoration to many. Yet again, her authenticity, humor, transparency, and passion for the Word come alive in this powerful book!"

—DARLENE ZSCHECH, WORSHIP LEADER,
HILLSONG CHURCH, SYDNEY, AUSTRALIA

"In NURTURE, Lisa so wonderfully reminds women of their tremendous capacity to bring life to others through the gift of nurturing. This book will ignite a desire to reach out beyond one's own weakness, pain, or inability and see the power of God within to help others find their own purpose and greatness."

—JOYCE MEYER, BESTSELLING AUTHOR AND BIBLE TEACHER

"Lisa has outdone herself with this book! This message is such an important one and the timing couldn't have been better. In her own unique and fresh way, Lisa tells us that we all need to be awakened to the call and responsibility of being nurturers. There are so many hurting, lonely people looking for what only we can bring. The kingdom of God is crying out for the women to boldly take their place. I dare you to read this book and respond to the challenge!" —HOLLY WAGNER, AUTHOR OF *GODCHICKS* AND
WHEN IT POURS HE REIGNS

"The idea of a woman being a nurturer has been lost in America and the daughters have turned towards other semblances to substitute for the emptiness in their lives. This is the tragedy I have seen that has befallen today's generation—a motherless generation. Lisa Bevere's NURTURE: GIVE AND GET WHAT YOU NEED TO FLOURISH depicts the value of nurture, one of the most important roles of a woman. Listen to her cry for change and make it happen! There is a battle to be fought and we need only to have women take a stand in their God-given role as warriors of the heart if we are to win it."

—RON AND KATIE LUCE, FOUNDERS OF TEEN MANIA MINISTRIES

"God's heart for humanity has always been to see them flourish and live in the expansiveness of His love, purpose, and plan. As God's Spirit moves quickly across the earth at this strategic time in history, many sons and daughters will respond quickly to the truths contained in Lisa's new book NURTURE. As one who sees firsthand the fruit and power of what a healthy, holistic, and nurturing environment can bring, I will be amongst the first to encourage many to read these wonderful, heaven-inspired words."

—BOBBIE HOUSTON, HILLSONG CHURCH, AUSTRALIA

"Lisa lives what she has unveiled in NURTURE. She is constantly instilling courage, hope, and confidence into others and particularly the next generation. We have lost the art and power of nurturing others and in this must-read book, Lisa inspires us to live in a way that ensures we are fulfilling this biblical mandate. Some of us lament that we ourselves may not have been nurtured, but rather than living in the pit of disappointment we can apply the principles in this book and be the nurturers for others that we wished we'd had." —CHRIS CAINE, AUTHOR AND DIRECTOR, EQUIP AND EMPOWER MINISTRIES

"Lisa Bevere's outstanding gifting and heart to see women's lives transformed shine through in this exciting new book. She speaks the truth with both passion and compassion—in such a wonderful way that many a life will be changed. If you long to thrive (and not just survive) as a woman who worships Jesus, then NURTURE is most definitely for you."

—BETH AND MATT REDMAN, WORSHIP LEADERS AND SONGWRITERS

"Lisa has raised her voice to express God's heart and God's call for women of all ages to connect and unite as never before. It's time for the baggage of jealousy, competition, insecurity, and fear to fall by the wayside as we reach out to nurture those who follow us—as we follow the Lord."

—NANCY ALCORN, FOUNDER AND PRESIDENT, MERCY MINISTRIES

"I enthusiastically recommend NURTURE. Women need to be nurtured—and they need to learn how to help nurture other women. Lisa offers loving direction, and her words have the potential to impact women in a significant way."

—BETTY ROBISON, COHOST, *LIFE TODAY*, FORT WORTH, TEXAS

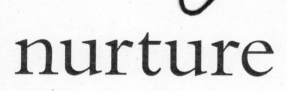

nurture

Give and Get What
You Need to Flourish

LISA BEVERE

Faith
Words

NEW YORK   BOSTON   NASHVILLE

Unless otherwise noted, Scriptures are taken from the *Holy Bible*, New Living Translation, copyright © 1996, 2004. Used by permission of Tyndale House Publishers, Inc., Carol Stream, Illinois 60188. All rights reserved.

Scriptures marked AMP are taken from the Amplified® Bible. Copyright © 1954, 1962, 1965, 1987 by The Lockman Foundation. Used by permission.

Scriptures marked The Message are taken from The Message. Copyright © 1993, 1994, 1995, 1996, 2000, 2001, 2002. Used by permission of NavPress Publishing Group.

Scriptures noted NKJV are taken from the NEW KING JAMES VERSION. Copyright © 1979, 1980, 1982, Thomas Nelson, Inc., Publishers.

FaithWords
Hachette Book Group USA
237 Park Avenue
New York, NY 10017

Visit our Web site at www.faithwords.com.

Printed in the United States of America

First Edition: March 2008
10 9 8 7 6 5 4 3 2 1

FaithWords is a division of Hachette Book Group USA, Inc.
The FaithWords name and logo are trademarks of Hachette Book Group USA, Inc.

Library of Congress Cataloging-in-Publication Data
Bevere, Lisa.
    Nurture : give and get what you need to flourish / Lisa Bevere. — 1st ed.
      p. cm.
    Summary: "Lisa Bevere teaches a new approach to mentoring that goes beyond encouraging to teaching important life skills."—Provided by the publisher.
    ISBN-13: 978-0-446-57759-5
    ISBN-10: 0-446-57759-6
    1. Motherhood—Religious aspects—Christianity. 2. Christian women—Religious life.
3. Mentoring—Religious aspects—Christianity. I. Title.
    BV4529.18.B475 2008
    248.8'431—dc22   2007028269

*This book is dedicated to every woman, regardless of age,
who longs to make her connection with other women
and touch the world she lives in but does not know how.
You, beautiful one, are an answer, not a problem
and we need both you and your contribution.
May these words help facilitate what you need
to begin to see your life enlarged on every level.
May the God-gifted treasure within you flourish
as you find your voice and place as one among
the many women who even now watch for you.*

Contents

Acknowledgments

Thanks to the many beautiful daughters who have written and challenged me with questions all while surrounding me with support. You are a watched-for, powerful, and long-awaited generation of daughters—stay strong and free.

To my mother, Shirley, and to every other mother who has taken the time to lay down her life to bring forth life in the lives of others: thank you for your strength.

To my friends Bobbie, Christine, Laura, Katie, Tonya, and Jennifer, who have been such beautiful sources of laughter and support.

To Holly, my editor, thanks for sorting through the random fragments and constructing that which makes sense.

To my handsome husband of more than a quarter of a century, thanks for loving me well and laughing with me. You are my closest confidant. May each year find us more in love.

To my four amazing sons: I love each of you more than words can say.

1

The Search for Nurture and Connection

SEARCH (verb): A careful and thorough examination in order to find somebody or something.[1]

I write as a mother and daughter of our time. In light of this I open by examining a classic childhood tale of our time by P. D. Eastman, the book *Are You My Mother?* (If you are unfamiliar with the tale, I will paint it well enough for you to know my point.) It was one of my favorite bedtime stories. The winning elements of adventure, loss, humor, and comfort are woven throughout the baby bird's repeated questioning of an unlikely host of candidates. As I laughed at the silliness of the bird's escapades, my own life felt anchored and secure.

When the story was over, the lights were turned off, and I was kissed and tucked snugly into bed, I would sigh and smile to myself. Why? All was well. I would never have to search like my friend the bird. I knew who my mother was. She was the very one who read to me. How could this little bird be so silly and confused?

More than four decades have passed since that time and I see the story a bit differently. I now understand the reason for all the confusion. This baby bird had never *seen* what it searched for. I, on the other hand, had never known life without a mother. Sadly, we now live in a world that looks very different from the one I knew. For a moment I want to revisit this childish tale because I believe its simplistic story captures the cry of a generation of searching daughters and mothers alike.

The Baby Bird's Request

The story opens with a proud mother bird sitting in her nest on her egg. Suddenly the egg jumps! She is startled by the realization her baby will be here sooner than expected and flies off to find some food. As she is off gathering food, her baby breaks through its shell with one question on its mind: *where is my mother?*

> *Dilemma #1: Mother is looking for food. Baby is looking for Mother.*

After looking high and low, the baby determines it must leave the nest to find its mother. The hapless baby bird steps into thin air and falls a very long way to the ground below. The search is on. The bird begins its trek by walking right by its mother, who is busy wrestling a worm.

> *Dilemma #2: Mother too busy to notice Baby. Baby doesn't know what Mother looks like.*

How could this happen? The baby didn't recognize its mother because it did not know what its mother looked like. She is so focused on the worm, her child is all but invisible.

Walking on, the baby bird approaches a series of barnyard animals and poses the question, "Are you my mother?"

The first to be questioned is a kitten that only stares. Perhaps it wondered what a baby bird might taste like. The bird moves on.

Next a hen is questioned: "Are you my mother?" She simply answers, "No." You would think she could have been a tad bit more helpful.

A sleepy dog is approached and he elaborates some, saying, "I am not your mother. I am a dog."

Okay, at least the baby bird has a bit more to work with. It knows now it is not a dog.

Dilemma #3: Right question . . . wrong source.

Next there is a cow who seems a bit perturbed and answers the question with one of her own: "How could I be your mother?" (The fact it gives milk doesn't make it a mother.)

This causes the baby a bit of a crisis. Was the search valid? Did it even have a mother?

Dilemma #4: How do you know what you have not seen?

After a moment's pause it confirms, "I did have a mother, I know I did. I have to find her. I will. I WILL!"

The baby bird no longer walks, it runs. An urgency has been awakened! It races by a broken-down car realizing there is no life in the metal frame. It runs to the edge of a cliff; perched precariously the bird looks down into a deep canal and sees a boat in the distance and calls out, but there's no answer.

The bird lifts its eyes. A plane is crossing the sky. "Here I am, Mother," The plane travels on without slowing for even a moment.

Frantic, the baby birds sees a "big thing" coming its way and runs to meet it. Without a moment's hesitation the bird leaps onto the teeth of a giant, earth-moving vehicle while shouting, "Mother, Mother! Here I am!"

Then the "big thing" speaks: "Snort."

The baby bird makes its first identification. "You are not my mother—you are a Snort." Actually it is a crane. (This is the part I thought was hilarious!)

Immediately the baby knows the voice is all wrong! This was not his mother. It tries to escape but finds it's too late. The "snort" is on the move. The giant arm raises the bird higher and higher. Terror overwhelms as the bird realizes it cannot run or hide. It is completely at the mercy of the "big thing" carrying it.

Dilemma #5: The "big thing" is not the mother. The "big thing" is now in control.

The Snort stops. Completely undone, the baby bird closes its eyes and wails for its mother.

Suddenly, all the pieces come together. The "big thing" drops the baby into its nest.

Stunned by the impact, the bird opens its eyes wide. At that moment, who should drop in but the mother, worm in mouth! This time it is she who poses the question. "Do you know who I am?"

And most certainly the baby does! After reciting an entire list of what she is not, it declares, "You are my mother."[2]

Happy Ending: Wide shot of mother and baby cuddling in nest.

A Mother Is Born

Okay, so how does this childhood story of lost and found speak to us today? Well, let's break it down.

First there is an anxious expectant mother who does not know that babies need to first know their connection. This element is even more crucial than their need for food.

I remember when I gave birth to my first son, he emerged looking a bit perturbed. His birth had been stressful. After twelve hours of hard labor contractions, the doctor had grabbed his head with large, cold, metal forceps and pulled him out. What a completely rude introduction to our world!

He came into view wailing. He was whisked away and dried and bundled in a blanket. The efficient nurse handed the screaming one off to the father. I was still in the closing stages of delivery—afterbirth and many stitches. From my vantage point I could see John felt completely awkward and at a loss. He bounced the bundle up and down, but Addison only cried louder.

I felt utterly helpless. I was unable to move, but I was certain if I could just hold him close and speak to him, he would be fine. I asked, "Can I hold him now?"

"Not yet."

I asked and was answered the same way four or five times.

"I promise I will not drop him," I pleaded, yet the truth was I'd never felt so weak in my life. I was still partially paralyzed from the epidural. I was at a complete loss. Tears came to my eyes.

One nurse must have sensed my angst. She came over and elevated the head of my bed and arranged the pillows against the guardrails so I was barricaded in. I will never forget what happened next. The nurse walked over to John to retrieve my son. She spoke quietly to him while she walked over to place him in my arms. He was crying lustily, eyes tightly closed.

When I saw his swollen, bruised face I realized he had possibly had a harder time of it than me. I said, "Oh, baby, I am so sorry." Instantly he stopped crying and turned toward the sound of my voice.

The nurse said, "Did you see that?"

I had. My heart leapt...he knew me! He recognized immediately who spoke. I was the voice he had heard for more than nine months.

I took him in my arms and whispered, "It's okay, baby—I am here."

Addison was suddenly and completely calm. He opened his eyes wide and looked directly at me. I don't know how to explain it, but in that moment something opened up within my soul; another birth had taken place.

> *There is power that comes to women*
> *when they give birth. They don't ask for it,*
> *it simply invades them.*
> —SHERYL FELDMAN

I was a mother, this was my son. There was an immediate connection. His stare penetrated and enlarged my heart. It was as though he was searching and sounding the depths of me just as I was searching him. We both longed to know and be known. I did not want to stop gazing into his eyes. Even though he was battered and bruised, he was the most amazingly beautiful child I'd ever seen. He was perfect in every way. Everything else was lost to me.

My baby bird had answered... "You are my mother!"

After a while, the nurse suggested I nurse him to establish my milk supply. I remember scanning my surroundings and wishing the setting was a bit more warm and private. I felt a bit awkward, surrounded by IVs, monitors, metal rails, and strangers. What if I didn't have what my son needed? What if my breast was empty? I suckled him and it was not long before he fell asleep, safe, sound, and satisfied, completely exhausted at my breast.

What meaning does this mother-child connection have today? The sons and daughters must know, first and foremost, there is a safe and intimate connection for them in this vast expanse of Earth. All of us must know we are watched for and welcomed. This must happen if we are going to flourish, for without this link it is far too easy to lose our way.

Ideally this connection should first happen in our homes, and then again in multiple ways as we journey through life. If you have never experienced this, it is time you did. If you experienced a violation of safety or trust where you should have had nurture, it is still imperative that these intimate connections happen.

All of us must know we are watched for and welcomed.

It is the purpose of this book to help position you to make those heart and relationship connections. The sons and daughters must be surrounded by nurture if they are to thrive.

Alone in the Universe

Returning to our friend the bird, we see that it struggled to bust out of tight quarters only to discover it was suddenly alone in an immense open space. Shouldn't there be someone to say, "Welcome"? Who would introduce it to this world? Hadn't there been another outside the thin eggshell? Hadn't there been singing and shadowed forms? Where was the warmth?

I wonder, is it the desire to join others that lends each of us the strength necessary to escape tight quarters?

The baby bird enters life without any boundaries or guidelines. Perhaps this baby was hungry, but even more than food, it needed to know both who and whose it was if it was to feel safe. The first cry of this humanized bird was not "Where's the food?" but "Where is my mother?" *Shouldn't she be here? Didn't she know I was coming today? Wasn't she watching for me? I must know her if I am going to be safe.*

And another thing—where was the father? Why did the mother have to leave her nest to provide for the baby?

Okay, perhaps in real life, baby birds really want only food, but humans crave intimacy and closeness. Daddy birds provide for and protect their young—humans do not always, but that is another story.

Mothers help us discover who we are. You can't allow just anyone to define you. You should not ask just anything who you are or whom you belong to. You should ask questions only of those you know have answers. Nothing outside of an appalling lack of perspective could cause a bird to ask a cow, "Are you my mother?"

Perhaps the cow's question and indifference actually challenged the bird's right to a mother. Isn't a question of value raised here? In essence the cow said, "How could you think you belong to me? I am so utterly different from you!"

This disregard caused the bird to question all it thought it knew. Was it ever cared for? Wanted? Watched for? Loved? Did it belong? Was there one who was bigger and wiser who would know and understand what it needed? Who would protect its young life? Who would instruct it and, when the time was right, teach it to fly?

These are the very questions that drive our human quest for connection.

In an atmosphere of nurture, the answers are revealed. There are answers with true mothers. There is safety when true mothers enfold us, even if they are not sure they can answer all the questions. We need the comfort and assurance of their presence. The truth is, there has never been a more desperate need for the presence of nurture.

I know something of this urgency. I travel the world and see motherless daughters running from one thing to another, calling "Here I am," but far too often their voices go unanswered. They call out, but the mothers are busy and the earth keeps turning. These daughters are in our homes, school systems, marketplace, and churches.

The daughters are in every age bracket and everywhere women can be found. They range from beautiful young actresses to doctors and attorneys. They are pastors' wives who are surrounded, but alone. They are stay-home mothers, isolated and exhausted. They are college coeds and women in prison.

The "Big Thing" Happening Now

Just as the baby bird ran to what P. D. Eastman called "the big thing," I think motherless women are running to another "big thing" happening right now. There is a stirring, a gathering, and an awakening happening around the world. Women are rising to take their places. They are finding their voices and reconnecting with their hearts. In response to this, doors are opening to women. Nature itself is crying out for the nurture the women bring.

> *Nature itself is crying out for the nurture the women bring.*

I believe this timeless reconnection of mothers and daughters will happen with the helpful intervention of the "big thing." The "big thing" is networking us through technology so each of us knows we are not alone. The big picture is opening up before us: The world needs its women. The sons and daughters need their mothers. Women need each other.

We are heartsick and in need of intimate, safe connections so we can in turn heal and help others.

The problems are so big, the needs so vast, so that our response must also be intimate and enormous. Big government with big guns will not answer the human cry for safety and connection. We are heartsick and in need of intimate, safe connections so we can in turn heal and help others.

Just as the "big thing" was not the bird's answer, it is not ours. Our "big thing" is the facilitator of connections. The bird's answer was his mother. On a larger scale, nurture is an answer to people's needs for connection. I watch amazed as the voices of daughters are rising and linking together on TV, over the Internet, through books and every form of media. If we can all begin to speak the same language of nurture and strength, we will make the necessary connections. There is amazing power in speaking the same language. It makes the overwhelming and impossible...possible.

Look at what God said when the people in ancient times built the Tower of Babel:

"Look!" he said. "The people are united, and they all speak the same language. After this, nothing they set out to do will be impossible for them! Come, let's go down and confuse the people with different languages. Then they won't be able to understand each other." (GENESIS 11:6–7)

When the languages were diversified, confusion set in and they were unable to complete their tower. Perhaps at that time

God did not want all the people in one place. He wanted the inhabitants of Earth to spread out and fill it.

But that was long ago. We have filled the earth and live in a very different season. I do not believe this is a season when God is scattering people—I believe He is in the process of gathering. I believe God has connections for the daughters and mothers on every level, in the marketplace, in the media, in the home, and in the house of God.

This gathering of women, this hunger for nurture, is what drives me. I want to find the daughters and help them recover life and safety. I want them to grow so they can fly. I want to turn the heads of the busy mothers so they will notice the daughters who are searching. And I want to empower the grandmothers to lend the comfort only they know how to give so well. I want these women nurtured well, so they can in turn enlarge the lives of others—who will hear the cry of Earth's citizens.

As the years have passed the story *Are You My Mother?* has become more poignant than funny. Actually I hear the inquiry echoed worldwide as a generation of daughters search the faces of other women in pursuit of mothers. The quest is not undertaken just by infants, but by those who realize that they have in fact lost something of value. They have turned to many semblances and forms of mothers but found that these substitutes were all in fact lacking.

> *I want these women nurtured well, so they can*
> *in turn enlarge the lives of others—who will*
> *hear the cry of Earth's citizens.*

Some of these daughters were forced to fly from their homes before they had realized the strength of connection with other women. They are ever moving, but never resting. Having never been nurtured, they have no frame of reference on how to nurture others. Some were abandoned in the nest and had to struggle to live. Others were intimately injured in what was meant to be a place of safety. Even now these women are afraid to stretch forth their wings and fly.

Perhaps you are one of these. Perhaps you are a mother who would love to do something but do not know where to start. Perhaps you are a daughter who desperately needs a mother. Perhaps you are both.

Women are life and relationship connectors. Where is your connection? Daughter, where is your mother? Mother, where are your daughters? Sister, where are your friends? Grandmother, where are the younger women who long for your wisdom?

God is stirring those whose hearts are longing to see these loose ends tied up. These are connections we need to actively search out and begin to develop. Sisters, I believe it is our time. Nurture, the language of the feminine heart, is being restored as women arise, recognize each other, and begin to connect for strength and purpose.

2

The Power of Nurture

NURTURE (verb): 1. To give tender care and protection to a child, a young animal, or a plant, helping it to grow and develop. 2. To encourage somebody or something to grow, develop, thrive and be successful.[1]

What a beautiful description of what the daughters of God so desperately need to give and receive: tender care, protection, and encouragement. There is such a resonance in my spirit that this is in fact our season to grow, develop, and thrive. You see, regardless of our ages we are all still God's daughters and therefore children of His kingdom. Women—daughters and mothers—of all ages need to awaken and recover their capacity to nurture just as mothers and daughters of all ages need to be strategically positioned to both receive and transfer this indelible life force.

Are we far too busy surviving to make the time to assure that the tender lives surrounding us thrive?

The need is far more urgent than we have the capacity to know. I fear that in so many realms of life the expression of nurture has become a lost or neglected art form. Are we far too busy surviving to make the time to assure that the tender lives surrounding us thrive? And often we are far too guarded, wounded, and afraid to open our lives to the possibility of nurture from an imperfect other.

Why? Too many of us were intimately wounded and profoundly disappointed by those who were entrusted with just such a relational stewardship. We sought nurture and were instead oppressed, neglected, or controlled. This is what happens when humans have lost their heavenly connection and perspective. They fight to the death to defend their religious traditions while unknowingly resisting what God is doing now on the earth.

But take heart, beautiful one, we are in a different season and heaven is passionately and purposefully reconnecting with our wounded, war-torn earth and the people who inhabit her. In this season I believe the daughters of God will prove integral agents in this process of reconnection. The heart, beauty, love, and nurture of heaven must be revealed on and in our earth.

Nurture is not expensive—it is expansive.

It would seem that most parents, educational systems, places of employment, governmental entities, and even houses of God are set up merely to meet needs, not nurture the human heart. It appears this is all we have the time and resources for. But nurture is not expensive—it is expansive. The life of everyone enlarges when nurture is added into any of these systems for it is then that those in the organization will cease to merely function—they will indeed flourish.

The Nurture of a Teacher

I hope you have encountered the amazing treasure of teachers who truly love to instruct. They approach their subject matter with so much enthusiasm and joy that you immediately know that are not merely reciting information, somehow they are intimately connected with their subject matter. They invite you in and want you to love this facet of knowledge the way they do. In college I had an amazing Italian literature teacher. He was everyone's favorite at the University of Arizona because he made history come alive, and somehow I felt connected to those people who roamed the earth so long ago.

Another teacher who was constructed of similar mettle was my high school science teacher. He made chemistry and physics fun, so much so that I in fact wanted to learn in his class.

But quite possibly the best example of a teacher who nurtured me was my freshman college English composition teacher. Sadly, I don't even remember her name. At that time my major was engineering and I was in her class only because it was required. Believe me, I was doing only the minimum that I could get away with and still pull a B. She loved writing and compositions. I hated both.

Her assignments were always the last that I poured any of my effort into. My science, engineering, and math classes required so much of my time that I waited until the last moment and began my English work very late at night, when all I wanted to do was go to bed. Whenever possible, I wrote in such a way that I did not use any sources so I did not have to go to the trouble of footnoting. I never did an outline or rough draft. I just wrote and turned in sloppy, random, marginal work.

But somehow she saw something in me that I did not even recognize in myself.

One day, after dismissing the rest of the class, she asked me

15

to remain behind. I remember that scary feeling in the pit of my stomach mixed with a bit of disappointment because I had wanted to walk with another girl to my next class. There were giggles and snickers as the other students filed out, laughing at my predicament. I did my best to put on my "I don't care" face as I slouched a bit lower in my desk.

The teacher came and sat down in the recently vacated desk next to me with my paper in her hand. "Lisa, I want to ask you a question," she began.

I was conscious that she was choosing both her words and position carefully.

I nodded. "Okay."

She spread the paper out before me and I noticed there was no grade on it.

"Did you write a rough draft?"

I shook my head and answered truthfully, "No."

"Did you make any type of an outline?"

I was feeling incredibly busted but there was something about her demeanor that made it safe to be honest. I sighed heavily and answered, "No."

"So you just sat down and wrote? How long did this take you?"

Okay, here is where I knew I was sealing the deal for an F! I began to falter a bit.

Sensing my nervousness, she offered, "Was it less than an hour?"

I nodded.

"Less than a half an hour perhaps?"

Okay—was my roommate an English composition spy?

"Yes."

She paused and looked at me. I was completely confused about where she was going. All I wanted was a passing grade! Distracted and a bit worried I would be late to my next class, I looked out the window and then back at her. I was hoping she would get to her point. Okay, I had turned in a sloppy bad paper. Point taken. I had another class to go to.

"Lisa, I can give you a C or a low B on this, but what I want to do is give it back to you and have you rework it."

Why in the world would I want to do that? Given my circumstances I thought the low B sounded like a great option.

She slid the paper my way. "You have a gift, Lisa, and I want to see you develop it."

Understand, I did not believe her for a minute. I was trying to figure out how I could work this to my advantage. I glanced down at the paper; though it was not graded she had circled some spelling and punctuation errors. How much effort was this really going to involve on my part? "Do you want me just to correct these errors?" I asked doubtfully.

"No, I would like you to rewrite it and develop fully what you began."

I agreed though I was still not sure what that would look like. I took the paper with me with the promise to turn it in next class period. I remember running down the stairs, out the door, and into the bright Arizona sunshine. Out on the campus mall I smiled. Someone had seen something in me that I had never seen in myself. I hated writing assignments! But she'd said I had "a gift." A seed was planted.

Over the semester I did try to rise to her expectations. I met with her a few times outside class to review my papers, then I moved on. I never took another English course after freshman composition in 1978.

She'd said I had "a gift." A seed was planted.

It wasn't until 1991 that all of this came back to me—and the seed she so carefully planted sprung to life. My husband was attempting to write his first book and struggling to transfer his thoughts to the written word. He knew what he wanted to say, but he was so bogged down in the writing aspect that he kept hitting a wall. At first we tried transcribing his sermons, but they lacked information John felt needed to be brought out. Then we hired an editor to write from John's speaking sessions and that did not work. Exasperated, John resigned himself to frustration and defeat.

My teacher's words returned to me and I approached John. "John, I can help you."

"How?" He was probably thinking, what could I do when two professionals had not been able to make this happen?

"I know your heart. Just type what you want to say without worrying how it is worded and I will do a rewrite." Then I added hesitantly, "John, I can write."

He looked back at me, puzzled. In our ten years of marriage this idea had never been discussed. "How do you know you can write?" John asked.

"Years ago an English composition teacher told me I could, but I never wanted to until now," I explained.

"Are you sure you want to take this on?"

"John, what do you have to lose? Give me what you have and I will rework it while you are on your trip," I offered.

I watched as a mixture of relief and hope relaxed my husband's face. He left for a trip and I went to work, and when he came home he found his words rearranged just how he wanted them. To be quite honest, there are far better writers and editors than I, but not for John in that season of our young life.

The correction and the nurture that sweet, nameless composition teacher had released into my life thirteen years earlier had reached into my future and spoken to me when I was ready to hear them. In college her words were corrective and directional, but when I met them in my future they were providential.

What Is Waiting to Be Awakened in You?

Beautiful daughter, pause a moment and think: is there some area you have potential in that is waiting to be remembered and developed? I know there must be.

Nurture has the power to enlarge or awaken areas of your life that will make significant contributions. Any gift, ability, or talent we have is given to us to improve and enhance the lives of others. There is something within you that this world desperately needs.

Empty-nester mother, there is something waiting for you in this season. This is not a season of loss; it is a season of transition, release, and expansion.

Single daughter, this is not your season of waiting; this is your season of discovering who you truly are.

Grandmother, this is your season of perspective and recovery. Everything you would have done differently in raising your children begin to put into practice with those beautiful grandchildren.

> *There is something within you*
> *that this world desperately needs.*

Children truly learn what they live. If mothers do not nurture their children, they raise sons and daughters who are self-focused, self-contained, disconnected survivors. These are individuals who have the capacity to function but lack the power to flourish. They are not unlike our houses that increase in size but for all their growth, never become homes.

Without the element of nurture, our culture fosters children who consume vast amounts of resources without ever truly giving back. They take time but rarely spend it. They receive money but are afraid to give it. They marry only to divorce. They laugh and make fun of others but rarely experience joy. They are expert critics who can break everything down for you, but they know not how to construct. They pursue peace but rarely apprehend it.

Without the element of nurture, our culture fosters children who consume vast amounts of resources without ever truly giving back.

For the most part their cultural heroes are superficial reflections of their own greed. Why? Because no matter how much money or how many cars, friends, awards, and accolades they receive, they are never enough to cause their pieces to connect or their lives to truly merge with those of others. They are far too busy taking what is theirs, protecting what is theirs, demanding what is theirs, and misusing what is theirs. Unless these breaches are addressed and healed, none of us will truly live the lives we were created to express. No one is isolated from greed and its rebound, poverty.

We were made for so much more than the meeting of needs, but if this is all we were given it is what we learn: *I need*. Remember the baby bird who wanted connection, but the mom was too busy wrestling the worm. Our human relationships degenerate to merely the meeting of needs rather than the melding of minds and hearts.

We Need Something More

And truthfully, we are not really meeting needs well. The poor are not cared for and the individual soul remains selfish. It appears all are afraid to give too much of themselves away. We have wives who grudgingly meet the needs of their husbands. There are husbands who do the bare minimum to meet their wives' needs. Parents scurry around busily meeting their children's needs. Employers strive to meet the needs of their employees. Employees strive to fulfill the needs of their employers. Teachers labor to meet the legislated minimum of the students. Government meets the welfare needs. The house of God meets the people's needs. Everyone is going through the motions and checking off their lists, but is this really living?

> **As royal, divine ambassadors we are to build heaven's relationship with the inhabitants of Earth.**

Are we truly connecting? Are we thriving? Do we actually know the people we live and work with? Do we know whom we teach? Do we know whom we learn from? Who is it that we worship with?

Where are tender care and encouragement? Where is evidence of flourishing? We are called to more than need-meeting, we are called to build lives and relationships. As husbands and wives, we are to love and foster a dynamic where both men and women flourish in their sacred relational connection. As mothers we should pursue a heart connection with our sons and daughters in order to form an intimate bond that secures them with love. As royal, divine ambassadors we are to build heaven's relationship with the inhabitants of Earth.

The Power of Pruning

People do not grow beyond themselves if they think the world revolves around them. I am not encouraging coddling or indulgence, but nurture. For far too often, what people want is contrary to what they need. This is Jesus' approach:

> *He cuts off every branch of mine that doesn't produce fruit,*
> *and he prunes the branches that do bear fruit so they will*
> *produce even more.*   (JOHN 15:2)

Pruning is a viable part of nurture. Branches that do not bear fruit are removed so the nutrients are not diverted to those that ultimately prove unproductive. Branches, which support the development of fruit, refreshment, and seed, are pruned or cut back so there is future abundance.

If you have ever experienced pruning in your life, you know the process is neither fun nor attractive. But being cut back is quite a bit different from being cut off. One is a complete removal from the source, the other is a conditioning so the life force of the vine flows more freely and efficiently through the branch and an explosion of fruit can happen.

Pruning can happen in a number of ways. A gardener can cut back branches, a passerby may absentmindedly break off branches, or a storm may clear the vine of brittle branches. Even you can sever what is unhealthy in your life or in the lives of your children.

I have a grapevine wrestling its way up the stone columns under the deck of my house. Its twiggy fingers have attached themselves not only to the columns but every time I turn around, they are strangling an innocent bush. In the summer I spend a lot of time gently unwinding the coils and relocating the branches to the columns. There they tangle and wrap themselves in themselves as they reach upward and outward.

I have noticed these trailers produce little or no fruit. When I lift their small and infrequent leaves, I find stunted clusters rarely as large as peas. Where I find the richest clusters of grapes is on the sturdier branches near the base of the vine. These close branches flourish and each season they are heavy with juicy, purple grapes. They are weighty while the unruly ones I failed to prune do little more than flap and wave in the breeze.

> ### *If a vine doesn't get pruned when it is young and tender, it will not flourish when it is older...unless the problem is readdressed.*

To be honest, the sad condition of my grapevine is entirely my fault. The first few years I allowed it to establish itself around the perimeter of the column. I was more concerned with its placement than its fruit. But after it was established I was the one who neglected to cut back the braches at the end of the season. I let them all stay in place because the snow came early and I didn't want to mess with pruning in subzero temperatures! I was also concerned about exposing the newly cut branches to the harsh Colorado climate. In the spring, I will have to do what I neglected in the blush of autumn.

The nurture of plants can encompass many phases and seasons, but if a vine doesn't get pruned when it is young and tender, it will not flourish when it is older...unless the problem is readdressed.

I can hear the reasoning of my older sisters: "No one gave me the tender encouragement and nurture I needed when I was young, so it is too late and too difficult for me to give those things to others." Don't believe this for a second. It is a lie. Why does God quicken each and every one of us through the process of rebirth? In this way we each are brought back to the beginning, regardless of our calendar year or season.

You have already been pruned and purified by the message I
have given you. (JOHN 15:3)

If you have been reborn, the Word of truth prunes your flopping branches. Divine nurture wants its way in your life. Incorruptible seed was planted in your heart and your life was pruned through repentance when you received the truth of His life-transforming message and became a daughter of heaven. You can in turn nurture even if you yet need some training in how best to do it.

Jesus' Story of Seeds

To produce good fruit, you begin with good seed. In the parables of Jesus, the seed was never the problem; it was poor soil or heart conditions that did not foster healthy growth. Some fell on a footpath and never sprouted before the fowl of the air pounced and devoured it. Other seed fell in shallow, warm soil and sprang up quickly but wilted under the heat of the sun because the roots found no sustaining nourishment (nurture) in the shallow soil. Other seeds grew among thorns that choked them and kept them from producing any fruit. The last group of seed found deep, fertile soil and multiplied into a harvest of thirty, sixty, and even one hundred times what was sown. Jesus explained the symbolism this way:

The Son of Man is the farmer who plants the good seed. The
field is the world, and the good seed represents the people
of the Kingdom. The weeds are the people who belong to
the evil one. The enemy who planted the weeds among the
wheat is the devil. The harvest is the end of the world, and
the harvesters are the angels. (MATTHEW 13:37–39)

Where are the weeds planted? In among the wheat! There was not a separate patch of ground designated for weeds. In my yard the weeds always go for the well-watered areas where they spring up quickly in an attempt to crowd out the seed I've planted.

One way to avoid this is to landscape so densely there is no room for weeds to slip in among the plants. But when you are working with seeds, it is a bit more difficult. For example, with wheat you can't always tell if the plant is bad until the time of harvest. This is why you still nurture the whole crop until the wheat can be safely separated from the weeds. Even God does this. He is good to the just and unjust until the appointed day of harvest.

Use Your Opportunities

Nurture can come in many forms and faces and if you didn't get it when you were young, it is important that you find it when you are older. It is just not an option to live without nurture if you want to flourish. The youth rising among us are just bold enough to walk up and ask us for the nurture they so desperately need.

Nurture can come in many forms and faces.

Therefore we who are more mature need to be on the lookout for them. We should be prepared with wisdom and the Word of truth and be ready to bless them in whatever ways we can.

Recently I had just such a moment with one of my sons. The encounter was so tender...even though it took place late at night. I was so tired I almost missed the opportunity. My sons had returned long after the actual close of the youth service. I was up waiting to lock up the house. I go to bed once I know everyone is home and heading in the same direction. As I turned off the downstairs lights, my son Alec called to me, "Mom, I am so sorry it's so late, but can I talk to you?"

Okay, I am closer to fifty than forty and at this stage of life sleep is a treasured commodity. I glanced at the clock—it was almost eleven— but when I turned back to my son he looked so earnest I couldn't say no. "Sure, come on," I said as I shuffled into the master bathroom. I am not sure why, but we have our deep private discussions there. "How was your group today?" (In addition to the youth group, my son is also a part of a smaller accountability group.)

He lit up. "It was amazing!" Alec answered enthusiastically as he settled into the vanity chair and I plopped onto the floor. That was when I noticed there was a scroll of sorts rolled up in his hand.

"Hey, Mom, do you want to see this?" he asked as he un-rolled the small piece of paper. He showed me his name and how he'd drawn each letter into a symbol that spoke to him.

"Each picture represents a portion of who I am or what I am called to do."

I listened as he excitedly relayed some of the highlights of his day and his group's interaction. I heard a list of who was there, what was said, and other details were filled in here and there to set the stage.

"Craig talked about our purpose. He shared with each of us some things he saw in us—our strengths and some other things God showed him to say." Then Alec shared some specifics Craig mentioned about him. As I listened I somehow remembered lis-tening to John many years ago when my then-young husband was attending Bible college nights and working in the field of engineering during the day—so earnest, so hopeful.

Suddenly Alec's attention seemed to shift from his day and he focused his attention completely on me. "Mom, what do you think I am called to do?"

It was a moment—a very important one—and I knew it.

Here was my beautiful son, so young, so pure, so sincere and impressionable. Late at night, looking for his mother's affirmation, he desperately sought after the heart of God. He gazed intently at me, his big brown eyes wide open to every possibility. Completely vulnerable, he was daring to ask, "What do you see in me?"

In the instant of this encounter I realized Alec's possibilities were limitless. I could fathom his life stretching and expanding so much farther than John's and my own. I hesitated because I knew what I said would go directly to his soul.

I told Alec I never wanted to limit what God had for him with my parameters. I shared how he was quite possibly called in a way I had never seen modeled here on Earth. I found myself almost afraid to say too much, to paint a picture too precise or construct a box too small. You see, I believe he is destined for signs and wonders. Beautiful one, I believe the same of you.

Where We're Headed

How great are His signs, and how mighty His wonders! His kingdom is an everlasting kingdom, and His dominion is from generation to generation. (DANIEL 4:3 NKJV)

To be honest, the signs I presently see are promising, but I would not go right to "great." I don't even know if I can say I have witnessed a mighty wonder. It would be a stretch. But where we are and where we've been is not where we are going.

God's kingdom is not a stagnant entity. It is an everlasting, ever-expanding catalyst of increase and growth. This kingdom will have no end. Please don't think of this as a function of time—it is not. Since when has our God been bound to time?

We will not have arrived when we get to heaven, we will simply have begun. There will be no possibility of a limit or barrier on heaven's horizon, no concrete wall or edge of the universe—simply a realm without end from a God who has no beginning. If one thinks on it too long, she gets lost. Our human frame and earthly life span can hardly prepare us for the immenseness of eternity. God is limitless and He wants His children positioned in the same manner. It is time the perspective of heaven came to Earth.

> *God is limitless and He wants His children*
> *positioned in the same manner.*

"What do you see in me?" is the question of every child. It is the inquiry of every daughter as well. If not posed to a mother, then it is posed to a father. If no one has ever shared an idea or impression of you that felt empowering and comfortable, you need to ask your heavenly Father, "What do You see in me?" He will whisper an answer that will enlarge your life and perspective on every front.

Please understand, we are not nurturing when we limit our children to what *we* have seen and known. We are altogether wrong if we set them up to expect too little. Don't position them by way of fear, worried that if we position them for more they may be disappointed. Perhaps you were disappointed and want to spare them the same pain...don't. Living small is not healthy or safe. Our children inherit either our fears or God's promises.

The disappointment we have seen—that is our story, our

world, our outlook, not theirs. Their stories may be quite unlike our own. Their lives may resonate with a new sound and be framed in an utterly different fashion, it might require a different set of lenses with which to perceive what they will steward. We may require a telescope to glimpse what is ahead, but they are moving so quickly they may well need radar!

Living small is not healthy or safe. Our children inherit either our fears or God's promises.

What Do You Reflect?

More often than not, we are mirrors for our sons and daughters. They peer into our faces hoping to catch reflections of themselves.

What will they see reflected in your eyes? In your words? In your embrace? I want to give you a window into the life of a daughter. Listen to her voice and feel the valid need.

When you call me "beautiful daughter," I feel like there is a hope and a future for me. Even though you are hundreds of miles away, I can hear you say what you write. It is like I am young again, and you are a mother who has cupped my face gently in your hands and is so very gently saying these words to me.

Do you see how little it takes, but how deep the love and nurture reaches?

They want us to look into their young lives and behold promise and be proud of them. Sometimes it is captured in moments such as the one I had with my son, and at other times it is reflected in multiple and flitting scenes that occur each day. I don't want my sons to be limited to what they have seen in us.

Nor do I want them to feel pressured or experience comparison with their parents.

As mothers and fathers, we exist for our children's benefit and strength—they do not live for ours. They are not placed in our care for us to live through. They were given life so they would go beyond our boundaries on every level.

> **The truth is I fear my life is not vast enough to capture the promise and potential of God's sons and daughters.**

You see, the truth is I fear my life is not vast enough to capture the promise and potential of God's sons and daughters. I seek to position but never limit, to inspire but never designate, to be an advocate without ever tampering with the God seed within. I pray to bless and never curse. Have you seen these sons and daughters? They are beautiful, fearless, and strong.

> *Our deepest fear is not that we are inadequate. Our deepest fear is that we are powerful beyond measure. It is our light, not our darkness that most frightens us. We ask ourselves, Who am I to be brilliant, gorgeous, talented, fabulous? Actually, who are you not to be? You are a child of God. Your playing small does not serve the world. There is nothing enlightened about shrinking so that other people won't feel insecure around you. We are all meant to shine, as children do. We were born to make manifest the glory of God that is within us. It's not just in some of us; it's in everyone. And as we let our own light shine, we unconsciously give other people permission to do the same. As we are liberated from our own fear, our presence automatically liberates others.* —Marianne Williamson[2]

What a beautiful portrayal of the child of God. Each and every one of us is a potential carrier of God's glory. We can walk out heaven's wonder and brilliance in the form of our varying earthen vessels. The time is long past for our lights to shine free and unhindered by religion and fear. To our shame, we have cloaked ourselves in the restrictive garments of lies and functioned in the land of the limited for far too long. Do not transfer these garments to the daughters. They will not wear them well and you will answer to God for hindering them with weights unnecessary.

> *"Yes," said Jesus, "what sorrow also awaits you experts in religious law! For you crush people with unbearable religious demands, and you never lift a finger to ease the burden. What sorrow awaits you!"* (LUKE 11:46–47)

Heaven Is Watching

Heaven and Earth watch as these sons and daughters step into view and their stage is the world. Why do you imagine the planet has become such an intimate theatre? Has there ever been a time when its inhabitants were so connected, when information was traded so freely and images transferred so effortlessly? We must decide whether these connections will be made for health and life or for death and destruction.

Was there ever a time when good and evil were so obviously in conflict? Even now our own roles ebb and flow, as we are both the audience and members of the cast.

> *Here am I and the children whom the LORD has given me! We are for signs and wonders in Israel from the LORD of hosts, who dwells in Mount Zion.* (ISAIAH 8:18 NKJV)

God is watching for a people who will answer, "Here I am, but I have not come alone. I come with children who are gifts from the God of Heaven and Earth." I love the exclamation point in this verse! Daughters of heaven, we need to be excited that we are not for rules and regulations but for signs and wonders in our world.

Wherever we find ourselves on this earth, we are for the declaration of His wonder and demonstration of signs that heaven is invading Earth.

Different Seeds = Different Plants

Any mother with more than one child understands they are all different. They are each uniquely crafted and formed for the glory of God, which is waiting to be revealed through their individual packages. There is freedom for both mother and child when we stop trying to make our children conform to image.

It is both fun and liberating when we celebrate their differences. They will all learn differently, love differently, and even obey differently.

A different kind of plant grows from each kind of seed.

(1 CORINTHIANS 15:38)

We are to create an environment that encourages them to realize their full potential—an environment of nurture. Each seed requires slightly different specifications of soil, moisture, and light if it is going to flourish.

**There is freedom for both mother and child
when we stop trying to make our
children conform to our image.**

We come into this world as seeds, not plants. In order to find our destinies and the destinies of our children, we must connect with some nurture. Nature alone is not enough to get us there—humans were made for companionship. When a seedling first appears, it looks much like the other seedlings. A translucent stem pushes two tiny leaves upward, then they unfold before the light. At this stage it is very vulnerable: the stem can easily be snapped, so all the factors of light, temperature, moisture, and soil nutrients must be balanced. If these elements are out of sync, the seedling will grow too high and spindly, and then the stem does not have the girth to support the leaves when they open. Once the plant is established it takes time, often many seasons, before it can produce fruit, which reveals its identity.

> *I planted the seed in your hearts, and Apollos watered it, but it was God who made it grow.* (1 CORINTHIANS 3:6)

God alone quickens life within each of us and causes it to grow. He gives seed to those He calls to sow and moisture to those who are to water. Still others prune and harvest. How can we practically apply these principles to impart nurture into the lives of those around us?

To answer, let's draw again on the definition of nurture.

Nurture Defined and Applied

1. Tender Care

Use this approach when you're handling sensitive areas or dealing with the young. Tender care is a genuine interest and concern coupled with a gentle approach as you tend areas in or instruct the life of another. We are charged to be tender with small children because their spirits are so pliable. There is never a need to be harsh when someone looks up to you.

> *Brothers and sisters, we urge you to warn those who are lazy. Encourage those who are timid. Take tender care of those who are weak. Be patient with everyone.* (1 Thessalonians 5:14)

Tenderness is also required when dealing with those who are injured. If you are rough, they will not heal properly.

2. Protection

This quality is often hard to navigate. We live in a mind-your-own-business world. But the truth is, as Christians we are to be involved in each other's worlds. If we see others at risk or in harm's way, we should intervene to see that damage is prevented. If we are in fact one body, then we are not isolated, and an injury to one is an injury to all. To protect is to prevent harm or damage from occurring. To know when to get involved, I try to turn the story around: if I were in the other person's shoes, would I want someone's input? If so, then I speak up. Meddling is messing without the motive to help.

If we are in fact one body, then we are not isolated, and an injury to one is an injury to all.

3. Encourage

Over the years I have found this to be the most priceless gift you can give or receive. To encourage is to gift another with courage, hope, and confidence. The world is filled with those whose hearts are failing them. There is widespread fear of loss on every level. For you simply to tell someone you believe in him or her is huge. Encouragement is in its purest form when encouraging someone lends no benefit to you.

You can even encourage complete strangers. I remember receiving a publication in the mail that featured a beautiful young couple. I looked at the wife and something about her made me smile. As I flipped through the pages, I loved that her articles were relevant and her pictures were fun and free. I had never met her and was not sure how I even got on their magazine's mail list. I went to put the magazine down when I thought I should call her and tell her what I think. Why not!

I flipped through the pages, called the number, and got an answering machine. All of a sudden I felt a bit silly talking to the answering machine of someone I had never met, but I went ahead and left a short message telling her in essence, "Well done."

The next day I received flowers. The day before had been just plain awful for this lady. She had asked God for some form of encouragement and when she checked her messages . . . there I was on the recorder.

I had the privilege of encouraging her by phone over the next few months and then I met her in person! The call cost me so little in the way of time and effort, it meant so much to her, and then the relationship ended up enriching both of our lives.

This concept of nurture will set the tone and frame our reference for all the other connections we will discuss. Nature is in upheaval crying out for the daughters to reveal the heart of nurture.

3

Making Connections

Before we proceed, I feel it is important we define some of the feminine terms we will use throughout this book. Honestly, the more I know of women the more I love them. But as I researched these definitions I found the descriptions far from adequate. For example, one definition of "mother" is: "A stringy slime composed of yeast cells and bacteria that forms on the surface of fermenting liquids and is added to wine or cider to start the production of vinegar."[1] Can you believe that? Some definitions had some good synonyms, but unworthy descriptions. In contrast, "father" had a vast and worthy array of words and descriptions.

In answer to this I have constructed some definitions of my own that combine the proper descriptions and some of my thoughts. Let's take a look.

DAUGHTER (noun): A female offspring; a girl, woman, or female animal in relation to her parents. The male equivalent is a son. Analogously the name is used on several areas to show relations between groups or elements.[2]

The following are my additions: A daughter is her father's joy and her mother's treasure because she quickens the heart. An heiress, she was hoped for and is their hope for the future. As the potential carrier and bearer of life, she is human wealth. Her creation was God's altogether lovely crown of creation, the one who completes.

> ### *An heiress, she was hoped for and is their hope for the future.*

Daughters are the feminine form, which embodies love, beauty, hope, and tenderness. A daughter is smiles, hugs, and laughter. She is a seeker of truth who asks many questions, longing to know who she is. She is a friend and comfort in your latter years. A daughter is like a priceless pearl.

MOTHER (noun): A woman who has given birth to a child (also used as a term of address to your mother); "the mother of three children." A term of address for an elderly woman, the woman of whom one was born.[3]

In addition to the traditional definitions, I have found mothers to be those who lay down life to bring forth life—whether this is by way of natural childbirth, adoptions, or rescue. I have found mothers to be advocates for children and change, protectors, nurturers, and healers of the sick. They are the ones who respond to a child's cry in the night. They grow into masters at multitasking. A mother is one who feeds and sustains life with warmth and what beauty she finds. She is a wiper of tears, calmer of fears, tender of injuries, instructor, teacher, friend, and confidant who gives advice whether you ask for it or not! She is a woman with answers who will tell you who she is. ("Because I am your mother, that's why!") A mother is likened to the interior coating of a shell called the mother of pearl (more on this later).

GRANDMOTHER (noun): The mother of your father or mother.

Additionally I have found grandmothers can be the amazing ones who know and love. They are the "yes" to whatever you ask. They wear soft smiles and give even softer hugs. They are confidants and advocates for both mothers and daughters. Grandmothers are the givers of both practical and unnecessary gifts. They are guardians of perspective, secrets, and insight. They listen and pray as they watch over their children near and far. They have selective memories and give advice when asked. Grandmothers no longer ask who they are because they have discovered *why* they are. Grandmothers could be likened to the outer shell of the oyster that surrounds and protects what is precious within.

> ### *Grandmothers no longer ask who they are because they have discovered why they are.*

All the definitions I have painted I have drawn from the lofty and noble perspective of these feminine forms at their best. Now that I have complicated things, I want to run the risk of oversimplifying.

Daughters are growing, so they need to ask for things, such as connection, love, affirmation, and answers. The question "Why?" is often in their mouths.

Mothers are grown; they have answers, meet needs, give love, ask for obedience, and are often busy. The word "Because" is often in their mouths.

Mothers . . . lay down life to bring forth life.

Grandmothers have aged and almost embody maternal love and life answers, but they watch and wait as they ask for hugs and kisses. The phrase "Let it go, it doesn't matter" is in their vocabulary as they pat you.

More than likely, you have not always experienced these feminine forms on their truest and highest plane. But even so there are daughters, mothers, and grandmothers outside your genetic pool waiting to make a connection with you. I want to lend you a window into what this might look like.

What Connection Can Look Like

I was signing books after speaking at a Fight Like a Girl conference. A long line of women was snaking its way through the sunny lobby filled with lots of hugs and laughter. I had just finished hugging one woman when I made eye contact with a beautiful young blonde who stood before me. I immediately knew something was different about her. I experienced that strange, uncanny, déjà vu feeling. I thought I recognized her because the spirit within me was quickened.

Puzzled, I was about to ask her how I knew her when I noticed the trembling lower lip and tear-filled eyes. It was then that I knew what she would say even before she leaned in to whisper, "You have been a mother to me even though we have never met. You'll never know. . . ." Her words trailed off as I drew her into an embrace.

But I did know.

She leaned in to whisper, "You have been a mother to me even though we have never met."

I knew exactly how she was feeling in that moment. She did not need to say anything more. I held her in my arms while she cried. All the noise and activity around us faded away. After signing her book, I gave her my direct e-mail address. "This is for you. What you write will go directly to my laptop. Please understand, no one else will read it."

She wiped her tears and nodded as we hugged again.

There was a long line of women patiently waiting for books to be signed. I had to move on, but something had transpired in this encounter, a connection had been made on both sides. For my part, a daughter had been dropped into my heart.

The next morning when I woke, her face appeared before me. Actually even now I can still see her…beautiful, young, and afraid.

I was certain I would hear from her again and when I did, I needed to be there for her. It was not long after this that she e-mailed me. Her words were both timid and intimate. She feared I might not remember her, but of course I did. There were questions that needed to be answered. She needed the honest counsel of someone she felt was safe. Her own mother was not in a position to answer these desperate questions for her.

I answered as best I knew how. I did not take her words lightly because I understood she weighed my responses so heavily.

She was revisiting something dark and frightening and I had the privilege of holding her hands as she transitioned to the other side. She questioned herself, her discernment, her motives, her value, her ability to be a wife and mother, and her destiny.

The truth is I did not really tell her anything she did not, at one level or another, already know. I just lent her my strength so she could believe and realize she could trust what she already knew to be true deep within her soul.

She was doing what daughters were meant to do—she was

looking for answers. Daughters will ask questions. If questions are not asked and answers are not given, then no one grows and healthy perspective is lost. Mothers are meant to answer questions and find answers. Daughters keep mothers relevant and real if we will allow them to do so.

> *I just lent her my strength so she could believe*
> *and realize she could trust what she already*
> *knew to be true deep within her soul.*

As a mother of four sons, I understand a daughter is a treasure. It is one I will never have the privilege of enjoying long-term. I was not destined to raise one of these princesses from start to finish, but that does not mean I should not be faithful to touch the lives of those who drop in on me from time to time. It will take many mothers (and fathers) to successfully raise the daughters of this generation, just as it takes many fathers (and mothers) to raise the sons who now walk the earth. Their season of nurture may be short, but it must be potent and concentrated if this generation of promise is to accomplish the God-breathed destinies woven into the fabric of their beings.

Over the years I have had many young girls approach me. I love encouraging them to seek the living God and fulfill His mind-blowing plans for them. Some ask questions about how to break into writing, others want to "pick my brain" on various topics. That is all good and fine, but a daughter looks a bit different when you see her. She is not looking for a list of do's and don'ts. She is not searching for ways to make ministry dynamic happen—you can read various books to learn these skills. No, a daughter wants something a bit more. She wants to know if you think she has the heart and soul to make it. She wants a mother to believe in her. She wants to know if you recognize her when she looks your way. She needs to know she is something more to you than she appears to everyone else.

I have had this happen when I am standing before a crowd of hundreds. Out of a sea of faces I will find myself fixated on a few. These could be women my age, women who are older, or a daughter who is younger, but somehow in the midst of that large group there is an intimate connect. I look out over the audience and see a hunger in their eyes. Often there are tears, but almost always there is something about their countenance, which tells me they get what I am saying. I almost feel I am expressing their hearts and lending voice to their longings. Almost without fail, these very women will approach me. I will make eye contact with them and tell them, "I saw you. You were right there with me. God was speaking to you."

They will nod and often tear up, embrace me, and share what transpired.

It is important they know they were seen. Often I will feel compelled to whisper a prayer over them right then and there.

I don't know how to explain it, but somehow you recognize a fraction of your spiritual DNA within another person. I will think I recognize some girls and when I ask if I know them, they will tell me they have read my books. But it is not really about me or you. There is a seed of heaven in these women's lives that you as a grandmother, mother, sister, or daughter in the house of God must bless and rejoice over.

> **Somehow you recognize a fraction of your spiritual DNA within another person.**

This blessing needs to happen even though you may never have the opportunity to actually watch the seeds of their lives grow. It is a God-breathed relationship, which may last only for that initial moment or perhaps extend to a season spanning months or years. A prayer is breathed, words are taken to heart, a hug is felt, a gift transferred, courage imparted, a blessing received and, before you know what has happened...you are related. A heavenly link is formed.

We Are Related

Anyone who does the will of my Father in heaven is my brother and sister and mother! (MATTHEW 12:50)

Anyone who does God's will is related to Jesus—isn't that amazing? But the promise does not stop there; we are not only related to Jesus, we are related to others who are doing the will of God along the same lines. When God *relates* people, it is for increased personal strength, spiritual growth, and kingdom purposes. There is no reason for anyone to remain isolated and alone.

How do you make these links or connections? Find out God's will for your life and begin to do it! And in the process you will discover others who are related to you. People of similar interests and passions naturally connect.

> **When God relates *people, it is for increased personal strength, spiritual growth, and kingdom purposes.***

The truth is, we are all better through healthy connections than any of us are when we stand alone. Regardless of how these links happen (in person, through media, by book, etc.) or how you are related (mothers to daughters, grandmothers to daughters or mothers, or sister to sister, etc.), something just clicks because in the medium of an encounter you realize you are already joined.

An excitement is released when you find out you belong to

such a heavenly lineage and network. A synergy is stirred as we are connected with God's family on Earth. We were not meant to do life alone—we were meant to be part of a family on every level.

> *There is a connection to be made that attaches us to one another and to the purpose of heaven.*

With some we will be intimately connected like sisters. With others we may enjoy the closeness and bond of mothers and daughters. Still others may be like cousins or aunts and uncles, but the good news is there is a connection to be made that attaches us to one another and to the purpose of heaven.

Some of My Heavenly Connections

I have learned you cannot force these types of relationships. But don't let this discourage you, because it is natural for related people to relate. I remember when I met my friend Christine, I loved her right away. She was like a long-lost sister not only because she is funny (even though she is)—we just "got" each other... almost immediately. Conversation flowed easily, laughter came naturally, and neither of us had to explain what she was about because it was already understood.

My heart was already open to Christine because a beautiful mutual friend named Leigh had already declared the existence of a God connection. She knew both of us and recognized a common passion and bent to each of us separately before either of us knew of the existence of the other. When we actually met, it just felt like a fit.

Another example of this is my beautiful travel assistant, Jacque. I first noticed her when she was an intern at the church we attend. Whenever her group was leaving for a missions trip,

I would make a beeline to pray for her. The first time I spoke to the interns she sensed the connection as well. She began to volunteer at our offices and devour my books. Then one day she came to me and shared that it was in her heart to work with me. I agreed and hired her right then and there.

When John came home I shared I had hired an assistant. Mind you, he had been pressing me to do just that. He asked for her qualifications. I said I wasn't sure, I just knew she had my heart and I trusted her. She traveled with me for more than four years and when the time comes, she will spread her wings and fly.

It is not unusual for God-related people to connect more intimately than even blood relations.

It is not unusual for God-related people to connect more intimately than even blood relations. It is difficult at times to explain to my relatives why I do what I do. They don't always get it. I bet you have the same dynamic with some of yours. Then, in stark contrast, I can speak with random strangers on airplanes and they will break down and cry. So what does it mean to relate or to be related?

RELATE (verb): 1. To have a significant connection with or bearing on something. 2. To find or show a connection between two or more people... based on an understanding... or on shared views or concerns. 3. To tell a story or describe an event.[4]

The last version of the definition is my favorite—the idea of telling a story or describing an event. Isn't that beautiful? Could it be these connections happen because we are all meant to play a part in each other's story? Actually I have no doubt that this is exactly why this dynamic is in motion.

My "Mother" Golda

We have spoken of daughters—now let's speak of mothers and grandmothers. You see, even though I am a mother I am related to many mothers or grandmothers, some of whom I have never actually met. They are women who told their stories by living their lives in such a deliberate, intentional way that a beautiful portion reached out in word or deed and quickened the story written within me. Some women modeled the strength for which I lacked a frame of reference.

Sometimes it was not even the actual women who touched my life, but just the stories of their lives that quickened me. An example of this was the first time I watched the actress Ingrid Bergman portray the life of Golda Meir in the movie *A Woman Named Golda*. I saw the movie but once in 1982, and yet it still speaks to me today.

In this story of the Israeli prime minister, I saw something I could relate to: she was a woman of iron surrounded by men of steel, yet she never ceased to be a mother. Intrigued, I researched Golda and learned that she had wrestled with life's questions, settled her issues, and then set the course of her life. She wept and laughed with all her heart. She owned her mistakes and continued to walk steadily and surely on the path laid out before her. She had military power at her command but never allowed the power to strip her of compassion. (I am not saying she did everything right... what leader has?) Golda had a great sense of humor and clear direction and purpose, and she refused to negotiate with terrorists!

As I have traveled this course called life, I found all of these to be character traits worthy of every woman's attention and development. Golda fought tirelessly to establish Israel as a nation with safe borders. She made one of her most powerful and telling statements in response to the continual Middle East peace crisis: "We will have peace with the Arabs when they love their children more than they hate us."

She knew life was ultimately about relationships. Women get this. Golda also understood there would be no lasting peace through compromise. Peace will happen only when our world learns to value its seed more than its present hostilities and love more than hate.

She knew life was ultimately about relationships. Women get this.

Golda Meir died the year I graduated from high school, but her legacy lives on in international leaders like Margaret Thatcher and other female government officials the world over.

Here is a great example of her humor; she once told someone, "Don't be humble. You aren't that great." Only a mother can get away with saying something like that! Mothers help you learn to laugh at yourself. I think it is because in most cases children find it safer to make mistakes around mothers than fathers. Children should just know they are loved. The love issue normally seems settled with a mother.

Other Mothers I Have Known

A few other mothers nurtured me whom I actually met. The first of these was a little red-haired fireball named Daisy Osborn.

The first time I heard her speak, I was at once intrigued and frightened. She was like no other Christian woman I had heard before. While the other speakers at the conference were busy talking about wearing the colors of your correct beauty season, earrings, and Christmas wreaths, this woman spoke boldly about raising the dead and restoring the dignity of women!

Her home was the world and her vision of beauty encompassed more than I had even dreamed to look at. I still vividly remember the words and text she spoke on at that Saturday luncheon at a hotel in Dallas. She was living the gospel accounts that I had only read about on fragile pages of black and white.

Her passion and words challenged and awoke possibilities in me. Just sitting in the back of the room, I felt a fresh hunger and desire stirring within, and my capacity to believe God was suddenly enlarged. I was a young, single girl of twenty-one who was in the habit of leaving functions promptly when they were dismissed. But after Daisy was finished addressing this elegant group of Dallas women, I found myself lingering and wandering near her table. She was understandably surrounded by a group of excited women. I couldn't imagine speaking to her. What could I possibly say—"Hi"?

> *She was living the gospel accounts that I had only read about on fragile pages of black and white.*

I just felt compelled to get closer. The knot of people around her seemed to draw tighter as I approached, and that is when I saw her white blazer (funny how you remember those things) draped on her chair. If I could not make actual physical contact with her, I would at least touch something she had touched. I am not sure what I thought might happen in this interchange, but I still reached out and did it. I tried to act casual about it, but my pursuit was anything but. Perhaps in the folds of cloth there was something hidden for me.

Interestingly enough, as the years passed I read every book of Daisy's I could get my hands on. John and I married and a time came when I actually had the opportunity to spend time with Daisy. Not unlike the daughter I described in the beginning of this chapter, she recognized me. Something in her knew me. Perhaps it was the silly jacket incident, or perhaps it was because I had taken the time to learn her heart and honor the truths she had recorded in her books. Either way we were connected. Even as I read her words I glimpsed her hopes and fears and learned that when she had been in my season of life, she was not too altogether different from me.

When I was with Daisy, she always encouraged and nurtured the gift of God in my life. Each time I saw her she spoke words of assurance and wisdom that she dropped like precious jewels into my lap. Lessons she had learned through hardship and suffering she offered freely to me and honestly...I still treasure them. One of the most powerful things she said to me was, "Let your past be your teacher and your future be your friend." The greatest present she ever gave me was her belief in the calling on my life. She chose to see something in me that others had missed. Or perhaps it was hers alone to see in that season. Heaven only knows, but she loved me well.

The greatest present she ever gave me was her belief in the calling on my life.

Daisy Osborn had a passion and zeal to see each and every daughter of the Most High God free and empowered to fulfill her God-given mandates. Before dying, she touched lives all over the world as she proclaimed the power of the gospel of heaven. Overseas she had witnessed the dead raised, blind eyes opened, leprosy cleansed, and lame beggars walking. She released words of life and power and watched as the demon-possessed were made free—and yet she made time to encourage me. Perhaps she recognized in my frightened, timid, American form...a future spiritual daughter.

Others crossed my path as well. I remember one rather

funny incident. I was at a Christ for the Nations gathering, speaking at their women's conference. At the afternoon session Joy Dawson spoke on the fear of the Lord. I was there in the second row to listen. I had an amazing amount of respect for this pioneer of truth. I had never met her but had heard her interviewed on various programs. When she was finished teaching her concise, precise message, she gave an exam—she tested us with questions from the podium while we wrote answers at our seats.

I worked diligently on the test and looked up when I had completed each answer. On one such pause she *appeared* to look at me and even to give a little wave. Confused, I looked around. The chairs to my left and right were empty and there was no one immediately behind me, so, a bit sheepishly, I waved back.

The test continued then. When I looked up, Joy looked again my way and mouthed the words, "I love you." I was completely taken aback. Again I turned around. No one else appeared to be the recipient of her affections. So I mouthed the reply, "I love you, too." I think I might have even choked up a bit.

What was happening here? Did she know me somehow? Had she read a book or seen me on TV? I was completely overcome by such warmth from such a mighty woman of God. When the class was done I approached her, but as I came closer she did not seem to recognize me in the least. Then, all of a sudden, Joy's face lit up as a young girl came into view. The girl was someone who sat a few rows back from me.

This was the one she had been talking to all along! Okay, I felt like a complete idiot! I had almost embraced her...she would have thought she was being assaulted! I went back to my room and just laughed at myself. Was I so desperate for a mother connection that I was intercepting those sent to others? How embarrassing!

A few years later I had the opportunity to spend the day with Joy Dawson as she graciously poured her knowledge into a number of us who had gathered around her. She was kind enough to spend her entire day with us. When we first asked if we could come and visit with her, she took it to prayer before she would give us an answer. When God gave her the go-ahead, she let loose with her whole heart.

Her approach was straightforward and no-nonsense. We came with gifts and an offering that honored her time and labor in the kingdom, and she prayed heaven down on our individual forms of Earth. She warned us not to do anything foolish and then told us if there was ever an urgent need, she would be there for us.

So there was a connection to be made...I was just a bit confused about the setting and very premature with the timing! When the time was right, the door opened.

Mothers and Daughters in Desperate Need

I believe there is such a desperate need for healthy connections among women of all ages. Everywhere I travel, the breakdown seems increasingly evident. Far too many women are disconnected and isolated. Others want desperately to connect but just don't know how to see this happen. It may be awkward at first, but it must start somewhere. The mothers need to watch for daughters and the daughters need to watch for mothers, and when they recognize each other they need to take the time to make that God-breathed connection—at whatever level or opportunity it presents itself.

I have seen God use just a slight squeeze of someone's arm as I walked by as a confirmation to the woman I passed that the God of heaven was in fact with her. You don't always have to speak—make eye contact, nod, wave, or smile. We all want to be noticed, acknowledged, touched, and drawn in. In light of this, the house of God is where we should always feel as if we are embraced, safe, warm, and sound. But our nurture should not be confined to the Christian realm. We need to reach out and touch others every-where we go.

So many daughters are out there watching and waiting to be seen, desperate to be noticed by a mother in the house of God. We need a host of just such mothers to deliberately watch for them, pray for the revelation of these daughters, and when they are found, hug them, affirm them, instruct them, and send them on their way equipped and empowered. Prayer is only the beginning; we must act as well.

So you see, faith by itself isn't enough. Unless it produces good deeds, it is dead and useless. (JAMES 2:17)

We must *do* something and respond to the needs we see. The women we encounter may not need literal food and clothing, but they desperately need truth and strength. (If they do have physical needs, those are, of course, the most urgent!) We must wrap them in splendor and feed them the bread and honey of God's living Word.

> *Our nurture should not be confined to the Christian realm. We need to reach out and touch others everywhere we go.*

It is not enough to intercede if you do not recognize or respond to the needs of the daughters who cross your path each day. We at Messenger International have developed resources specifically for women so they can open their hearts and homes to daughters of all ages who are hurting. If you bring others into the safety and intimacy of your home, God can do such amazing feats of healing. So many God-breathed resources are available now that there is no excuse: it is easier than ever to do the Father's will.

There is such incredible power to open and close the hearts of those you encounter just by deliberately choosing to connect. Oprah is an amazing communicator because she connects on so many levels with both her audience and her guests. She is intentional about connection and a host of isolated men and women know it. She is there to raise awareness and lend strength, but she doesn't leave it there; she empowers people to do something with what they have learned.

If this can happen in a studio and over the television, why can't this happen in our homes? Why not in the house of God? Is it because far too often people feel safer isolated in their homes on their sofas than they do in our church pews? What about connections such as these happening in the marketplace? What about in schools? What about in our homes?

Pearls and Their Mothers

We opened with definitions; allow me to close with an illustration. A few years ago I was in Hawaii. I woke to a rainy, gray morning with the words *mother of pearl* in my mind. You almost can't turn around in Hawaii without bumping into a pearl booth, but I had never given much thought to the "mother of pearl." I wandered down to the on-site pearl jewelry store. Because of the weather, the store was empty and a kind clerk sat down and opened a pictorial book and answered my questions. What I learned that day opened my eyes and gave me a beautiful perspective on motherhood and the beauty of nurture.

Pearls are amazing. Pearls grow the best in the pristine waters of Tahiti. There each element of nature joins together to orchestrate the birth of beauty. It is interesting that pearls are referred to in almost strictly feminine terms. There is the term *mother of pearl*, or Pearl as a female's first name. The very shell that houses the pearl as it forms almost resembles a womb.

The formation of a pearl is the response to a seed or irritant lodging itself within the confines of a mollusk (oyster or mussel). The mollusk isolates the irritation and coats it in successive, circular layers of nacre or the mother of pearl. This eventually results in the formation of a pearl. This process continues for as long as the mollusk lives.

You see, the irritant or seed creates a wound in the lining of the mollusk similar to the way an embryo "wounds" and implants itself in the lining of uterus. The response to the wounding is that something new and beautiful begins to grow. In the womb of a woman a life is quickened and the body responds immediately by creating interior conditions to foster its growth. The interior of the womb heals over the "wound" the fertilized embryo caused and this connects the seed with all it needs to grow and flourish.

If you look at the interior of an oyster shell, you will see the color range of the mother of pearl. You will discover shades ranging from the black of onyx to luminous white. This encompasses various shades of gray, lavender, pink, and yellow you may see between the bands. It is interesting that each pearl does not reflect all these colors. No, just one hue is captured in all its glory.

The mother of pearl has many colors, yet she transfers just one shade to her daughter, the pearl, in seamless perfection. The individual pearl reflects one facet of the mother in her luminous globe of convex beauty. The mother cradles this daughter within the safety of her shell, all the while adding layer upon layer of luster until the time comes when the daughter is released from the confines of the shell.

Likewise the beautiful, luminous form of a child grows within the safety of its mother's womb until the time of birth. They say the uterus is the strongest organ in the human body, yet its strength develops involuntarily. The uterus expands for nine months as it retains and sustains life within, but in the fullness of time it begins to contract progressively and rhythmically until the child is released.

The response of the pearl holds this hope, that what was painful to the mothers can become a thing of priceless beauty in the daughters. Let's allow them to be coated in glorious luster by learning and responding to the issues of life well.

What was painful to the mothers can become a thing of priceless beauty in the daughters.

Could it be that the twelve gates of heaven, each made of one giant, luminous pearl, represent the feminine contribution to the twelve tribes of Israel (Rev. 21:21)?

> *The Kingdom of Heaven is like a pearl merchant on the lookout for choice pearls. When he discovered a pearl of great value, he sold everything he owned and bought it!* (MATTHEW 13:45–46)

In the next chapter, let's explore further what a sister-to-sister connection looks like.

4

Sister to Sister

SISTER (noun): 1. A girl or woman who has the same parents as another person. A close woman friend, especially of another woman. (adjective) Belonging to or closely associated with something.[1]

What is the deal with sisters in the Bible? As I scanned the Bible, I found 357 matches for *brothers*—quite a few of these described friendships—and only one hundred references for *sisters*. Most of those were just family designations beginning with "And the sister of Tubal-Cain was Naamah" and closing with "Greetings from the children of your sister, chosen by God."

These references do not hold much to aspire to. Actually as I reviewed them I could not find one single story of females who managed to connect in a healthy, functional way. In the New Testament you have the sisters Mary and Martha, who bickered and fought over kitchen duty and the attention of Jesus. In the Old Testament you have the sisters Leah and

Rachel, who were married to the same man. Not what I call functional!

There was also no record or mention of healthy friendships between women who were peers. You may argue, "What about Ruth and Naomi and Mary and Elizabeth?" They were not peers, they were older and younger women. Understand I don't believe this lack of connection between female friends exists because the Bible does not value relationships. There are frequent references to and stories of male bonding and friendships, whether the men were related or not. These brotherly alliances were frequently formed through shared experiences or hardship. It would appear there is a strong sense of brotherhood and a nonexistent or weak, not-worth-mentioning sisterhood. You just rarely find the women uniting or expressing friendship with peers in a deep and meaningful way. They more frequently appear as jealous rivals jockeying for position and affection! Again, this is not a relational model I want to copy.

Upon discovering all this, I had to ask: Why? Were women never meant to be friends? Why don't we celebrate one another? Are we best left isolated and alone in our individual homes? In the house of God are we to have no place set at the table of communion? Or are we invited to sit but not to interact? Or could it be that there is a connection and dynamic with women—related by blood or not—yet realized?

Frustrated, I cried out to God and this is how He answered: "The chapter of the daughters is being written right now. Tell My daughters to write their lives well."

Tell My daughters to write their lives well.

As I pondered this, I remembered this verse from the book of Acts:

I told you... about everything Jesus began to do and teach.

(ACTS 1:1)

Jesus began something we have the privilege of finishing by His Spirit. Do you understand what you have been born into? We are in the season of restoration and recovery for God's daughters! Just as the men formed alliances around fields of battle, it is time we rallied around causes of our own. This is not just a churchwomen dynamic. It is a connection for every woman in every walk of life.

Recently John and I went to an air-band contest at my son's high school. The majority of the audience was composed of young females. There were ten groups competing, two of which were female. I watched as the girls in the audience cheered enthusiastically for the boy groups and barely condescended to clap for their fellow females. The contrast was so glaring that my husband turned to me and asked, "Why don't the girls clap for each other?"

"They just don't," I whispered back.

It appeared he was noticing this lack of female support for their gender for the first time. I nodded knowingly. After the show John and I went out of our way to compliment the girls who had entered the competition. They were clustered awkwardly and almost appeared ashamed. In contrast, the male air-band groups were boisterously congratulating each other and arguing about who should have won what. I reached out and touched the back of one of the girls, saying, "Great job! I was glad to see some girls up there."

John echoed his affirmation: "You guys were great!"

They looked back at us doubtfully. "Really?"

"Yes," we assured them, but they looked far from convinced. They had sensed that the female audience had not supported them and had actually just wandered off the stage at the end of their act. While all the other groups had jubilantly celebrated their triumph to the sound of loud acclamations, these daughters had looked lost.

Sisters, we need to start clapping for one another! Mothers need to clap for daughters. Mothers need to applaud each other. Daughters need to lend some props to the mothers. Daughters need to cheer for each other. Everyone needs to clap for the grandmothers! Why do we want to withhold support from each other? Are we that threatened and insecure?

Sisters, we need to start clapping for one another!

Jesus is not coming back for a church or even an army. He is coming back for a bride. This lovely end-time metaphor that captures and embodies His relationship with the church as a whole will one day be collected without spot, wrinkle, or blemish. We need to make sure she is not covered with the scratch marks of catfights.

Make Ready the Bride

Bride is definitely a feminine term, which implies women need to get busy and be part of the process! I mean, what bride would trust her adornment to a manly man? In the Bible only eunuchs (men who could not reproduce) were given access to the women in this intimate manner. It is women who adorn the bride with beauty. It is women who counsel her with whispers, tears, and laughter, as questions are raised and matters of the heart revealed. It is women who performed the ancient ceremonial washing to purify and renew. It is sisters who arrange her hair and apply the elements of makeup that enhance her beauty. It is women who gather the flowers and release the fragrance. It is women of all ages who congregate to shower her with gifts of all kinds so her home will be filled with beauty, good food, love, and laughter. It is women who share intimate advice to allay fears and stir her passion. In the parables, it was the wise virgins who arose and lit the bride's way with plenty of oil in their lamps when the trumpet sounded the bridegroom's arrival. It is women who share both a bride's joy and longing as they charge her to allow love to rest until the appointed time.

> *It is both our privilege and mandate to celebrate and prepare the bride for the coming Bridegroom.*

After the Cross, it was a cluster of women who tenderly washed, anointed, and wrapped the body of Jesus in preparation for His burial. Tell me, who else was entrusted with such intimate access at so vulnerable a time? I can see them gently handling Jesus' lifeless body as they washed His battered frame with fragrant oil and tears. Had the disciples ever touched Him in such a way? Certainly they had jostled Him, but only women were ever allowed to caress. And it is women who once again will lavish their affection and adorn His bride. Adam has once again laid down his life that Eve may come forth in joy. It is both our privilege and mandate to celebrate and prepare the bride for the coming Bridegroom.

Women: Warriors of the Heart

We have been painted a prophetic picture of what must happen. To see this type of beauty transferred, our current female relationship model must undergo a drastic change! Please understand, with this issue I truly know in part and I prophesy in part. I have yet to see the whole realized. We are in this season of flux as the body of Christ collectively expands to breach the gaps that currently exist. In our day and hour there yet remains a tension between the way things are and the way they should be. God always makes these adjustments from the inside out. Who better to begin this process with than the women? Are we not the ones who are used to expanding to bring forth life in the process of pregnancy? Even now the church is pregnant with mothers and daughters.

Again, from the very beginning, women were afforded intimate access to Jesus. We were there when the angel announced Emmanuel and the Virgin Birth. We were there as His life was quickened within Mary so that one day it might be quickened within us. Tell me, what man has ever known what it is to be pregnant? We were there in the throes of childbirth. We were there to suckle and nurture the child Jesus. We recognized the Christ as an infant in the temple. We were there anointing Him in the midst of judgment and religion as the fragrance of spikenard from an alabaster box filled a crowded room filled with men. We were there at the foot of the cross as He suffered and died. We were there in the tomb. We were the first to witness His resurrection while His male disciples hid in fear.

Women have always been intimate partners with the redemptive plan of God. It is now our time to partner in His return.

Men plan wars but women plan weddings. Both are on our horizon—it is time to make ready.

Men plan wars but women plan weddings. Both are on our horizon.

Men may most frequently govern the nations, but it is women who guardian the heart. (And yes, I believe women can govern the nation as well!) Know the heart is more powerful than a nation. What government has ever held the power to change the human heart? You can control the actions of people by limiting their liberties, but you cannot, with all the outward restrictions, chain the heart. Kingdoms rise and fall as time ebbs and flows, but the heart is forever. God alone knows the heart and has the power to truly change it.

What begins in our hearts will eventually spread to our lives, fill our mouths, and overtake our actions.

Women have intimate access to the human heart to influence it for good or evil. What begins in our hearts will eventually spread to our lives, fill our mouths, and overtake our actions. The corresponding deeds have the power to impact individuals, collective groups, and eventually nations. If the heart is healthy, its warmth spreads to all it makes contact with.

Both Genders Are Needed

Do you see why the enemy of our soul wants women isolated, oppressed, and afraid? If we are fragmented and powerless, the heart of the bride remains broken. The light of her beauty will not draw others if she has turned her gaze within. Participants in weddings are not self-focused, they are focused on their beloved and joyously anticipating what will be. Meditate on this in context of the following prophetic verse:

> There will be heard once more the sounds of joy and laughter. The joyful voices of bridegrooms and brides will be heard again, along with the joyous songs of people bringing thanksgiving offerings to the LORD. They will sing, "Give thanks to the LORD of Heaven's Armies, for the LORD is good. His faithful love endures forever!" (JEREMIAH 33:10–11)

Men and women were made to laugh together. The voices of the sons and daughters are to be raised in uncontainable joy, explode in song, and spill over into laughter. This expression should not be contained.

In this word picture men and women laugh together as both declare God's goodness and never-ending love. But this declaration is not isolated to a church building—it flows out into the streets and is heard by all! There will be such joy when both the voice of bride and Bridegroom, sons and daughters merge to declare God's amazing love and mercy. Far too many have lost this innocence and joy and, in the process, lost sight of God's goodness.

Men need women. The daughters and sons together capture the fullness of God's image in human form (Gen. 1:27). The men are the strength and the women the heart. Might without heart or compassion can be cruel, just as a heart without authority is weak and vulnerable.

How to Make Meaningful Connections

So beautiful daughters, where do we go, when our hearts are hurting, lonely, and isolated?

Of course, we first cry out to our Father. This means we are brutally honest about our needs and desire to be connected to the other daughters He is awakening. We ask Him what needs to happen so we can be healthy within these connections. This is where He sifts our motives, so we approach this process through the avenue of truth. In His presence He will call us by name and commission us in our areas of strength. Then we need to gather with those who are like-minded. These are women with whom we are compatible or on the same wavelength. This will lend us insight and cause us to turn from ourselves and reach out to others. I understand this is often difficult to accomplish, but it is imperative that you connect with healthy, passionate, beautiful, free, and godly women.

I have a group of women who are just such a treasure in my life. I am very much a newcomer to their circle because they have all been friends since college. It has only been in recent years that I have had the privilege and blessing of being invited into their lives.

> *He will call us by name and commission*
> *us in our areas of strength.*

We are a core of six with an occasional seventh or eighth floating in and out. Each of us is a wife, mother (collectively we have twenty-eight children), and woman in active ministry with her husband. Three are pastors, two are mission leaders, and still another is a voice to the youth of our nation. When we are together, we drop all titles and job functions and remember this is our time to gather as God's daughters.

We live in three different states and one is outside the country, but we make it a priority to get together at the onset of each year. We converge on Sunday and part ways on Tuesday. During this short time period we laugh, cry, confess, exhort, play, and pray together. We discuss anything and everything in a safe, nonjudgmental atmosphere. When the need arises, we get involved in each other's lives and sometimes even enlist the help of our husbands. As we gather, we share the triumphs and struggles of our past year. We ask questions, share answers. We don't always agree but we respect our differences of opinion and perspective. God has always answered the prayers we have lifted before His throne as we cluster in our circle and pray over each other.

We all want to do life well and we want to do it in relationship with other women. We have all lived long enough to see those who began well and ended up really stupid. Who wants that? Some women are outspoken, others speak softly; some hail from completely functional households, others from a bit of the dysfunctional vantage point. Each of us has different strengths and perspectives, but somehow in this group we are all related.

The first time we congregated in Dallas, I was a bit nervous. I knew only one of them. What if the others did not like me? What if I was an awkward fit and threw the whole thing off-kilter? Far too often I had been a bit of a loose cannon in the female dynamic, and I was almost at the point of giving up. But Katie, the one who had so thoughtfully included me, was so kind and gracious that I knew if the others were anything like her there would be no problem.

As we found our seats around the circular dinner table, we each shared who we were and what we hoped to glean from our time together. It was a bit uncomfortable at first, but necessary. We needed to know who was present and why. If we didn't do this, we wouldn't feel safe. As we spoke, the conversation became increasingly intimate. No one sat back and observed...we all leaned in to listen. A few hours passed and the lights dimmed in the restaurant as the glow of candles warmed our faces.

Questions were raised that none of us knew the answers to. We all agreed to search out truth and reconvene knowing more the next year. The plight of the young daughters was addressed. Would we be intentional and search them out in our churches and other circles of influence?

Finding the Daughters

What would that look like? Our own lives were so full, but we brainstormed. Each of us was aware of the need and the weight of responsibility now in our laps. It was our season to reach out—how could we not respond? Some of us admitted we were intimidated by the young girls and what they face. Most of us felt ill-prepared to address the needs, but all of us agreed to allow God to open our hearts to His possibilities.

Before we left the table that night, an unusual thing happened. Jennifer, the beautiful brunette who sat across from me, said softly, "I knew we would be friends, Lisa." Her face was illuminated with a warm smile.

I must have looked puzzled, so she went on to explain, "I saw you a few years ago on television and I was so convinced we would be friends that I actually wrote you a letter, but I never sent it. I did not want you to think I was some weirdo and I felt strange about explaining myself, so I just dropped it. I said to myself, *I like her and if she ever meets me . . . she will like me, too!* And now here we are."

And of course she was correct. I did like her. It was such a welcoming embrace, but its warmth was extended not just to me—it is for you as well.

Do you hear this? Other women are watching for you! They want to be your friends. They are just not sure how to approach you. Perhaps they are at your school. Maybe there are women searching for friends in the marketplace. I know the daughters in the house of God are looking for companions. Women the world over are looking for someone who will understand their hopes and fears as only another woman can.

> ### Do you hear this?
> ### Other women are watching for you!

Open your eyes and look around you. I believe God is in the process of connecting His daughters with each other, with mothers, and with grandmothers. He is establishing relationships and family dynamics among His people. This is where we will find our places of strength. As we link together, weaknesses will be minimized and assets maximized. You see, my friends see things in me I often miss in myself. They watch for the best. They know me well enough to realize I am far from perfect. But because we are sisters, they still recognize our Father's hand on my life.

We lend importance to others
when we listen intently.

I tend to see myself through the eyes of critic and judge. I am intimately acquainted with my failures and can be very hard on myself, but when I am with my sisters they will not let me go there. They are too busy lifting my vision and lending their strength. I see them in the same light. I value each of them because each is an answer to my prayers.

The heartfelt counsel of a friend is as sweet as perfume and
incense. (PROVERBS 27:9)

Heartfelt counsel is a rare treasure. It is hard to find those beautiful friends who are both earnest and honest. The perfume of such an encounter has the power to scent or fill a room. It is an aromatherapy of sorts. Remember, fragrant incense is a form of prayer and thus a connection with the divine.

Where two or three gather together as my followers, I am
there among them. (MATTHEW 18:20)

As we gather, it is important we don't just talk; it is equally important we come together to listen. Sometimes it is incredibly healing simply to know that we have been heard. I was recently part of an altercation where reason was not working. In the midst of it I heard the Holy Spirit whisper, "Just listen—they need to know they have been heard." We lend importance to others when we listen intently. What does it hurt for you to listen? Even if we don't come to a conclusion or resolution, there is comfort in knowing others listened and understood...even if they did not agree. It is beautiful to be in an atmosphere where everyone is valued and invited to contribute her portion.

I once had an experience similar to Jennifer's. I was watching a music video and as the camera panned the front row of the church, I caught a glimpse of the pastors. When I saw the wife, she somehow looked like someone I should know. Had I seen a portion of myself in her? I rewound the tape and paused on the scene for a closer look. "John, she's a pastor and she looks like someone I should know—someone I would be comfortable with!"

I am certain John thought me a bit bizarre as I pointed to a tawny brunette who was worshiping God, eyes closed and arms outstretched. To be quite honest, until then I had a hard time connecting with images of women in ministry leadership. Their package seemed so different from my own. But that night more than a decade ago, when I saw her I realized it was okay just to be myself: free and lost in worship.

There is connection for all who dare to watch for one.

So much has changed in the last decade—women are so much more a part of ministry now—and there are hundreds if not thousands of such women on the horizon. There is connection for all who dare to watch for one.

Relationships Flow Naturally

Of course, relationships have to flow naturally. They cannot be forced. Our group joined together the next year as well. We had kept in contact, sharing kind words and encouragement when necessary. We exchanged gifts and cards and all of us anticipated gathering again.

When we met the second year (well, for me it was the second year) it was even richer and more dynamic. We all agreed other women needed to have an opportunity to connect in this manner. So we set to work on a plan. Each of us would invite six other women, and then we could have seven groups of seven. We made lists of discussion topics and invited an amazing mother/grandmother type to address us. We formulated a mini-invitation-only event for women in ministry.

The right thing at the wrong time is still a disconnect!

But it just was not the same. An amazing group of women came, so it wasn't because any of the pieces were wrong. It was just we did not all fit together comfortably at that moment. The intimacy and chemistry of our group of seven had been lost in the translation. We had all of the structure but lacked the heart connections; we had the format but not the function. It wasn't because of a lack of desire—every woman who came wanted to connect. But the range of perspectives and expectations in the group was quite possibly too vast.

You can't force these types of connections but you can foster them. The right thing at the wrong time is still a disconnect! God connections are made when the timing is right. If the timing is off, it is like trying to deliver a baby before it is full-term.

Everybody wants it to come forth, but if the time is wrong, the birth is just not going to happen.

Get Ready to Get Connected

How can we foster relationships? Look at this verse.

As iron sharpens iron, so a friend sharpens a friend.

(PROVERBS 27:17)

Notice it does not say "As iron sharpens steel," but "As iron sharpens iron." To experience a sharpening, you and those you gather with must be made of similar components. The package or form may look different, but friends are usually compounded with comparable elements and core beliefs. Therefore, when you come together there is a sharpening rather than dulling of your perspective. Your outlook is honed and your comfort zones are challenged. What is the purpose for sharpening an instrument? So it can be more effective or precise. Did you know you are more likely to be injured using a dull knife than a sharpened blade? Precise edges require less force and pressure to wield.

If you have ever been sliced by a dull blade, you know the wound takes longer to heal than a clean incision made with a precise cutting edge. We need to sharpen the edges in our relationships. The season of networking just to climb the social ladder is over. God is toppling these ladders. They are propped up against frail, man-made structures, but God is building His house with living stones that have been honed accurately and fitted together precisely.

And you are living stones that God is building into his spiritual temple. (I PETER 2:5)

Now is the time for us to prepare to be connected. God, our heavenly Father, is in the process of honing our individual stones so we can be built into a habitation for His Spirit and presence. This is imperative because none of us will be who we need to be without God-given relationships. Let's examine the reasons why women don't make the connections they so desperately want by reviewing some of the hindrances to this process.

Why Women Don't Connect

Envy

Envy (verb): To look with enmity, to feel pain, uneasiness, mortification or discontent excited by the sight of another's superiority or success, accompanied by some degree of hatred, usually with a desire to depreciate the person and pleasure when we see them depressed. Envy springs from pride and ambition.[2]

Now that we have defined this sabotaging emotion, we need to address it. Envy is unreasoning and senseless. Sadly, it is a widespread emotion among the daughters of God, one far too frequently used by the enemy of our souls to separate and destroy godly allegiances and alliances. God is far more powerful than our enemy and at times He flips the destructive course of this powerful emotion to accomplish His purposes. Please understand that envy is rarely satisfied unless its objective is destroyed. Envy is not after a relationship with you, it seeks your ruin. It wants your position in the Spirit, but this position in the Spirit is not yours to yield. It is God-given and has very little to do with you. He chose you, so don't allow this force to intimidate you.

*Envy is a symptom of lack of appreciation of our
own uniqueness and self worth. Each of us has
something to give that no one else has.*

—ELIZABETH O'CONNOR

Joseph's brothers envied his position of favor with his father, Jacob. They hated the fact he looked at life differently and would not be tethered to their small patterns of thinking. They were incensed—how dare he dream when theirs was a life of nomadic drudgery? How dare he check up on them when they were in fact the older brothers! They would put an end to his illusions of superiority. They would dash his dreams once and for all and cast him into a position lower than theirs. They would sell him into a life of slavery and despair.

But the truth is God used the envy of Joseph's brothers to actually promote Joseph so that he would one day be strategically positioned to save them all.

God accomplished the same type of dynamic with Jesus. Scripture tells us Jesus was crucified because of envy. We read of Pilate:

*He realized by now that the leading priests had arrested
Jesus out of envy.*   (MARK 15:10)

The priests had been harassing Pilates with complaints about Jesus for a long time as they repeatedly raised multiple charges against Him. But their opposition was never really about modifying Jesus' synagogue behavior or confirming His allegiance to Rome and Caesar; they hated Him because He was superior to them on every level and the people knew it. Samuel Johnson wrote, "Whoever envies another confesses his superiority."

In the Old Testament, Joseph's rescue of his people was the

foreshadowing of what Jesus would do for each and every one of us in the New Testament. Joseph's brothers had intended harm and destruction to Joseph just as the lead priests had intended harm and destruction to Jesus—but God intended good. How shocked the brothers (and priests) must have been to find the very one they were so envious of was the one who stewarded the answer to their gravest problem!

In the case of Joseph's brothers, it was food and supplies in a time of famine; for the priests, it was the sacrifice that would once and for all time take away their sins and the sins of all people. It would appear God flips envy to His advantage when it is necessary.

Jealousy

> JEALOUSY (noun): That passion or peculiar uneasiness which arises from the fear that a rival may rob us of the affection of one whom we love, the fear that another does or will enjoy some advantage which we desire for ourselves, suspicious fear or apprehension.[3]

This is a sister emotion to envy but there are some subtle differences, the most pronounced being that envy is a form of hatred and jealousy is a type of fear.

Jealousy injures us with the dagger of self-doubt.
—LESLIE GRIMUTTER

We are going to focus on its destructive nature, but jealousy can actually be exhibited in a godly form as well, such as when God was jealous for Israel's affections and Paul was jealous for the Corinthians' obedience. The Bible does not say "Love is not jealous," it says, "Love does not envy." Jealousy gone wrong can be a relationship destroyer.

Surely resentment destroys the fool, and jealousy kills the simple. (JOB 5:2)

Resentment and jealousy tend to run hand in hand. We look around and imagine the blessings and relationships others enjoy are the very ones we should have. But, beautiful daughter, this is just not so. There is a place for you at God's banquet table. There is no shortage of love, life, beauty, or relationships. There is richness to be found unless you are too busy eyeing the life of another, echoing the sorry words "If only. . . ." "If only" is a lie. You were not meant to live the life of another, you were meant to live your life with passion and gratitude. If it is somewhat less than you desire, it is up to you to rewrite your story or attitude; don't insert yourself into the story of another or try to steal the role he or she plays. We all need you to be fully who God created you to be.

The jealous bring down the curse they fear upon their own heads.

—DOROTHY DIX

Jealousy is a waste of time. Your wishing you had the life of another will not grant you any true happiness; instead, you will find yourself completely frustrated. In fact, no one truly knows the pains and joys of others. I have lived long enough to learn the lives I thought were ideal from my vantage point were often the emptiest existences of all. There are so many gorgeous, glamorous women who would give up all their fame to be truly loved.

We all need you to be fully who God created you to be.

There are enough relationships and friendships to go around. When we hold the relationships we have with another too tightly, we squeeze the very life out of them. We should all be protective of the health of our friendships and marriages, but not fearful. Fear is a really bad counselor —it always leads us in the wrong direction.

Please understand what I am saying. I am not encouraging you to be careless with your relationships. You should not be comfortable with your husband spending time alone with another woman. It is just not wise to put either of them in that position. It is not good for intimate relationships to be fostered with the opposite sex if you are married. But it is wrong for you to be jealous if your proclaimed best friend spends time with another. Be thankful her life is enriched by relationships with others, and don't make her feel guilty.

You never want to limit yourself to just one best friend. We need to have a number of friends who are the best for us in different areas. There are those who are best at giving advice, perhaps another is best at making us laugh, and yet another who is best at challenging us to transform into the God-people we are called to be. It is highly unusual that one person is the best at bringing all these things out in us.

We need to have a lot of friends who are "best."

This brings us to another hindrance to connection that is closely related to jealousy.

Competition

COMPETITION (noun): The activity of doing something with the goal of outperforming others or of winning something. Related words: rivalry, opposition, antagonism, war, struggle. Antonym: friendship.[4]

75

Benjamin Franklin said, "To find out a girl's faults, praise her to her girlfriends." Ben Franklin's comment is really sad, but I fear he is far too often proven correct! And look how long ago it was said—so for more than two centuries this has been an accepted truism. Isn't it about time the daughters of heaven changed this? We are not in a contest with one another. We are, together, in the midst of contention between dark and light. If we make a comment to lower someone in the eyes of another in an attempt to somehow level the proverbial playing field, we have slipped lower still.

Notice the opposite of competition is friendship. This illustrates true friends are not competitive with each other. Friendship should never be about what we do or have, but about who we are to each other. Most of us don't learn this truth until much later in life. If the young daughters can glean this truth early on, they will make healthy, noncompetitive connections in their friendship choices. You see, competition tends to exist when we surround ourselves with friends who make us uncomfortable with who we truly are. I am not saying it is wrong to have friends who inspire you, but it is wrong to befriend others because you want to study them in order to beat them in some form of wannabe contest.

The good news is there is more than enough room for us all! We are all needed if we are going to see this lost and dying world healed.

There is an Earth-felt need for someone just like you.

Yes, there is the amazing Joyce Meyer reaching out through media and crusades to touch the world. Did she compete with someone to get where she is? No. She saw a need for practical truth and chose to meet it. There is the sincere Beth Moore teaching God's Word through Bible studies worldwide. Is she trying to win a contest? No. She has a passion for God's Word. What about Darlene Zchech—did she win a praise-and-worship pageant? No. She loves God and wants to see others enter into His presence with joy and freedom.

There is room for many more. The spaces and places are not all filled. There is an Earth-felt need for someone just like you.

The next time a friend is complimented in your presence, simply agree—or better yet, add to the flattering description. You will in no way lose by doing so. If we can do away with the backbiting within the house of God, perhaps we will find we can be true friends to one another.

Gossip

> GOSSIP (noun): Conversation about personal or intimate rumors or facts, especially when malicious.[5]

Notice it is still gossip, even if it is a discussion of facts! Note to self on this one: just because it is true it doesn't mean I should repeat it. I am not professing to have this lesson down completely, but I have found some ways to limit the toll gossip has taken on my life. The ancient proverb our moms repeated is of course best: if you can't say something nice, say nothing at all. But sometimes you are saying nothing and someone else is talking! It is not cool to listen to gossip even if you don't add to it or pass it on. It still has the power to affect your perspective. So what are we to do?

Well, if you can't keep quiet and if your friends are going to be gossiping—be alone! There are times, many times in fact, when I have placed myself in voluntary time-out to keep from sinning. If there is no opportunity to say what you should not, then you can break the habit of loosing words that should never be given voice.

I have very strong opinions, but I also have a lot of influence so I have to be careful. What I say in passing may be weighed far heavier than I ever intended. What's a daughter to do? Again, say kind things. This will knock the wind out of both gossip and competition. Why would I ever be troubled if my words of kindness were repeated?

Fire goes out without wood, and quarrels disappear when gossip stops. (Proverbs 26:20)

Sometimes I will hear something someone said about my husband or my children and I will initially be furious—how could they say such things? I will want to pick up the phone and settle the issue right then and there. Trust me, it is best not to. Don't chase the tales a gossip carries. Some things are so ridiculous they do not even merit a response.

There is so much good in the worst of us,
And so much bad in the best of us,
That it hardly becomes any of us
To talk about the rest of us.
—Edward Wallis Hoch

Isolation

Isolation (noun): 1. The act or process of isolating.... 2. The quality or state of being alone: aloneness, loneliness, singleness, solitariness, solitude.[6]

Far too many women are alone. When you are isolated, your world revolves around you, your problems and perspective. This fosters excessive self-consciousness. We imagine everyone is looking at us and talking about us, because we are all we think about. The only cure for this is to realize the world is way bigger than we know. Take initiative and don't wait for others to approach you...approach them. Step out beyond yourself by getting involved in the lives of others. Invite someone over or to lunch. Offer to volunteer at a worthy cause, strike up a conversation with random female strangers at the grocery store. Practice reaching out until it just seems natural. I never used to talk to anyone, but now I sometimes have to forbid myself!

Men

MEN (noun): The male of the human species.

Okay, I am going to try to say this correctly: the number one thing that separates women is men. Mind you, this is not always the doing of the men, quite frequently it is the fault of the women. Women have been known to sell each other out for the attention of a man. Men are not usually that silly. Mature ones do not drop their friendships so quickly over a woman. Likewise we do not declare ourselves valuable by betraying or abandoning one relationship for another. We need our friends, both male and female.

> *If you just set people in motion*
> *they'll heal themselves.*
> —GABRIELLE ROTH

Women tend to betray each other because somewhere along the way they have lost their truer sense of self. Getting a man in your life will never be the end-all solution, especially if you are untrue to yourself or others. We'll look more at the issue of being true in the next chapter.

5

Be True

TRUE (adjective): 1. a. Consistent with fact or reality; not false or erroneous.... b. Truthful. 2. Real; genuine.... 3. Reliable; accurate: a true prophecy. 4. Faithful, as to a friend, vow, or cause; loyal.[1]

I hate it when I have been untrue. I hate it when I discover I've been lied to. It just makes me feel sick, but the following sonnet speaks of a subtler and yet even more destructive deception—the breaking of trust with one's self. If we are going to move into the realm of nurture, our course must be genuine.

> *This above all: to thine own self be true, and it must follow, as the night the day, thou canst not then be false to any man.*
>
> —WILLIAM SHAKESPEARE

At first glance Shakespeare's words seem a given. I mean, who would knowingly lie or deceive herself? But my fear is women are frequently vulnerable to self-deception, which means, of course, they do not even realize they are in fact false with themselves. Because they are untrue to themselves they are false with others without even knowing it. In light of this dynamic, our friend William raises a few points worthy of closer examination.

True to Self, True to Others

First, when we are true to ourselves, we will naturally or innately be true to others. If false to ourselves, we will inevitably be false to others. Of course it stands to reason that if our core or center is "untrue," then we cannot consistently release or communicate truth to those who are around us. Why? Because like it or not, we release what is within us.

If we want clarity and truth, then our murky waters must first be purified if they are to be found clean and true. If a source or core is tainted, all that issues forth from it is likewise polluted. When it comes to the human dynamic, the heart is the place where truth is secured and falsehood confronted. In reference to the heart and its outflow in the form of our words, James posed this question:

> *Does a spring of water bubble out with both fresh water and bitter water? . . . No, and you can't draw fresh water from a salty spring.* (JAMES 3:11–12)

Daughters, it stands to reason that if the source or well we draw from is salty or untrue, then the water we pour forth is likewise unwholesome. Out of the abundance of our hearts our mouths will speak. Saltwater looks refreshing until you try to ingest it. An even more telling example of this is found in these words of Jesus:

> *If the light you think you have is really darkness, how deep that darkness is!* (MATTHEW 6:23)

This represents the power of self-deception, a mire of deep darkness. If your choices and actions are driven by darkness and deception, like will produce like. A darkened heart is filled with confusion and fear, but it imagines it is filled with light and direction. The good news is darkened places can be enlightened by the revelation of truth and the muddied can become crystal clear once again.

> *There has never been a more desperate need*
> *for faithful guardians of the heart.*

Returning to Shakespeare's proverb, when we are true to ourselves, or to our hearts, then we are true to others and likewise safe stewards of their hearts. Proverbs 31 describes the virtuous woman as one who could be safely trusted with the heart of her husband. I believe this guardianship could be extended to every relationship a woman carries in her life. She is a trustworthy guardian of the hearts of her children, of her friends, of her community, of God.

There has never been a more desperate need for faithful guardians of the heart, but none of us will navigate this precious stewardship well until we have made peace with our own heart condition. I know more than anything else, you want to be a true daughter, a true friend, a true wife, and a true mother. I, too, want to experience the true life of Christ on every level of my being, so over the last year I have had to ask myself some hard questions about matters of the heart.

No Part Dark

You see, in this God way of living there can be is no coexistence or mingling of lies and truth. If something is 99 percent truth and 1 percent a lie, it does not qualify as true.

Therefore take heed that the light which is in you is not darkness. If then your whole body is full of light, having no part dark, the whole body will be full of light, as when the bright shining of a lamp gives you light. (LUKE 11:35–36 NKJV)

There is to be "no part dark." Daughters, I know you are tired of hearing lies, speaking lies, supporting lies, and ignoring lies. But are we really truly ready to stop living lies? When this desire to be true overtakes us and actually transforms our actions, then our reputations as daughters of the Most High God will radically change. We may not be known as "quiet and sweet" but we will be known as "meek and true." (My mother always warned me about the sweet ones!)

No longer will we be known as daughters who wander aimlessly in and out of the realm of good and evil as we try to make "good" choices. We will have risen to so much more. When His daughters are heart-driven, they will behave as residents of the realm of God.

No one is interested in joining the club of the fearful and powerless nice women.

Only then can we act as ambassadors and representatives of heaven's light and beauty even while we tread the shadowy paths of this earth. When we walk in this manner, those who surround us will be drawn to His light and power within us. Yes, it requires power to live in this world but not be of it. No one is interested in joining the club of the fearful and powerless nice women, and no one wants another recitation of our endless list of rules and regulations.

What Light Does

You are the light of the world—like a city on a hilltop that cannot be hidden. No one lights a lamp and then puts it under a basket. Instead, a lamp is placed on a stand, where it gives light to everyone in the house. (MATTHEW 5:14–15)

Do you hear what Jesus called you? The light of the world! Think on this declaration a moment. Is this how you would describe or represent yourself? He is no longer here as the Light of the world, and this is not just a bonus Christian name. He needs you to be this—light! Jesus is in heaven with the Father. He left this privilege of being light-bearers to the sons and daughters who yet inhabit the earth. It is absurd and just plain wrong ever to enclose or encase the light within us. The illumination of life within should be elevated for all to see.

There has never been a more desperate need for this beacon to shine freely for all—especially for those who most need nurture—must perceive and draw near to its warmth. When people find themselves in gross darkness, they naturally gravitate toward the safety and assurance of light...unless, of course, it is hidden.

Light is amazing. Watch a newborn baby: their gaze will always turn to light and faces. Babies are irresistibly drawn to both. Light has the awesome power to reveal surroundings. It also can expose what is hidden within. Light invites others to gather in its glow as well as warns of danger, as in the case of a lighthouse. Light within warns us as well. Because it is indispensable, why and how do we hide our light?

How We Obscure the Light

I believe one way is by suppressing the truth within us. This happens as we cover our glow with vessels powerless to magnify its radiance. This dulling down or filtering can happen when we use Christianity to expound rules rather than exemplify relationship. The bushel basket comes down hard when we espouse judgment and law rather than mercy and truth. If we place lights on the ground and superimpose our Christian grid of "good" over the beacon, we risk losing a large portion of our original freedom and brilliance. Do you remember when you were first saved, how easy it was to discern between light and dark? Then somehow along the way, the more you knew, the more muddled it became?

A few of my boys are rather enamored with fire. There have been various unauthorized experiments conducted in my home involving matches, aerosol cans, and candles. For a moment let's imagine what might happen if an open flame is covered with a basket. Depending on the density of the weave and length of time, one of two things could happen: the flammable basket could catch fire and potentially cause damage, or the flame could slowly be snuffed out and die.

When we cover rather than exalt the light, we lose its visibility. If the covering is flammable we run the risk of vessels' catching fire. In this example, the light Jesus refers to is one given for illumination both mental and physical, not the fire we might kindle for warmth.

Sometimes we suppress the truth by telling ourselves, "Great, you are a daughter of the light! Wonderful! Now here is a list of rules—memorize them well." You have just been moved from the inward leading to outward conformity. In the days of Paul it took the form of enforced circumcision, head coverings, and Jewish laws. Frustrated with the Galatian church, he said,

> *How foolish can you be? After starting your Christian lives in the Spirit, why are you now trying to become perfect by your own human effort?* (GALATIANS 3:3)

It is my prayer the sons and daughters of God will throw off these awkward baskets, which even now obscure their portions of the light. The dynamic of revealed or uncovered light happens only when we are true to ourselves and are led by our hearts, not by some list of rules.

Human nature gravitates toward a checklist or outline of Christian do's and don'ts.

You see, the heart is often harder to read than a list and therefore human nature gravitates toward a checklist or outline of Christian do's and don'ts. But this list will inevitably cause you to be false with yourself. Daughters, never allow a written human code to separate you from what was written on your hearts! The elevation of the light to the height of a stand happens as we lift up Christ and He in turn draws others to Himself.

How Can We Be True?

So what does it mean to be true? We aren't true simply by telling the truth, for to "be true" encompasses so much more. To be true to yourself, you must be faithful, loyal, and honest with your heart. Only then can you provide nurture for those who need it. If married, you would not join your heart in allegiance to or alliance with another. Single or married, you would not allow what is false to gain entrance to your heart through what you hear, say, or do. The heart is the source of our new lives.

The definition of true appears at the beginning of the chapter, but the primary sense of the root word *true* is "to make close and fast"; related words include "faithful, trust, loyalty, fidelity, safe, secure."[2] This means we need to unite and tie together the truth within us so that the lies without will have no access. Immediately I think of the admonition in Proverbs:

Let not mercy and truth forsake you; bind them around your neck, write them on the tablet of your heart.

(PROVERBS 3:3 NKJV)

And again, in the New Living Translation this time:

Never let loyalty and kindness leave you! Tie them around your neck as a reminder. Write them deep within your heart.

(PROVERBS 3:3)

Notice how the Bible translators interchanged "truth" and "loyalty" and "mercy" and "kindness" in this verse? What is true and what makes us true is to be etched on our hearts. I have visited this verse for years but only recently did I question what it really looks like. So how do we write something on the tablets of our hearts? To find our answer, let's delve into the verb *write*. A few definitions are: "the transfer of data, to create or compose so others can read or listen to something, to reveal or exhibit clearly." But here is the one I found especially profound: "to ordain or prophesy what will happen in the future."[3]

Do you hear this? If the heart is transcribed with truth, it will ordain (proclaim and order) or prophesy (reveal God's will) in life. If your heart is on target, then your future is secure. This is crucial because most Christians know where they are going but they have no idea how to get there! The Word of God becomes the director of our paths:

Write the vision and engrave it so plainly upon tablets that everyone who passes may [be able to] read [it easily and

87

quickly] as he hastens by. For the vision is yet for an ap-
pointed time and it hastens to the end [fulfillment]; it will
not deceive or disappoint. Though it tarry, wait [earnestly]
for it, because it will surely come; it will not be behindhand
on its appointed day. (HABAKKUK 2:2–3 AMP)

God instructed the prophet Habakkuk to clearly display the vision God had given him so those who walked past it could see it for themselves. The appointed day is coming when what was written in our hearts will be revealed. But until then, there are promises and visions yet to be fulfilled. There are power and truth to proclaim. God is preparing His daughters to be glorious lights in this world.

Now is the time to sweep away the lies and lay hold of the truth.

As we hide the Word of God within our hearts through reading and meditating on it, it begins to transform us. Because the Word is a living force, it has the power to etch itself upon our hearts, purge, and speak to direct us. Have you ever noticed you remember Scriptures you have heard or read? Why? Because the Word's voice is retained within and speaks to you in the intimate recesses of the secret place...your heart. Conversely, if we can write truth deep within our hearts, then it stands to reason lies could be written there as well.

Now is the time to sweep away the lies and lay hold of the truth.

Mercy, truth, loyalty, and kindness are the attributes we are to transcribe on the core of our being. When this occurs, all we do will be driven or guided by those precepts. Self and the heart are intertwined. You may question, *Can I trust my heart, can I trust myself?* You must! When we are born again, our stony, deceptive hearts are removed and tender hearts of flesh are entrusted to our care. Hearts of flesh must be protected because even though they are more accurate, they are also more vulnerable.

The Realm of the Heart

Keep and guard your heart with all vigilance and above all that you guard, for out of it flow the springs of life.

(PROVERBS 4:23 AMP)

From our hearts, or our truest form of self, proceeds the very issuance of life referred to in Proverbs 4. Our hearts are truly regenerated when we are translated from the kingdom of darkness into the kingdom of light. It is taking a while for the rest of me to catch up to the renewal that began with my heart. Sometimes I have gotten confused along the way, but when my heart rather than my head drives me, then the way is clear.

The realm of the heart is where the daughters of God are to abide. We can no longer be directed by the rigid confines of the written outward code that governed our behavior when we were inhabitants of the kingdom of darkness. There is now a new and living way.

By his death, Jesus opened a new and life-giving way through the curtain into the Most Holy Place. (HEBREWS 10:20)

We are to be inspired and led by the Spirit, who breathes life and wisdom into our every situation. How does this happen? We listen to our hearts. How can we trust the counsel of our hearts? We wash them with the living water of God's Word to purify our motives. We fill our hearts with loyalty and kindness so they are closed to all other input and influences. Then we ask for God's guidance. Spiritually positioned in this manner, we are promised:

> *Then you will find favor with both God and people, and you will earn a good reputation. Trust in the* LORD *with all your heart; do not depend on your own understanding.*
>
> (PROVERBS 3:4–5)

God cannot resist daughters who trust Him with all their hearts.

Depending on our "own understanding" refers to being led by our heads rather than our hearts. The longer I have lived, the more I have realized my head will lie to me, but my heart rarely does. My heart has only misinformed me when I mired it down with self-deception, pride, fear, and offence.

> *Seek his will in all you do, and he will show you which path to take. Don't be impressed with your own wisdom. Instead, fear the* LORD *and turn away from evil. Then you will have healing for your body and strength for your bones.*
>
> (PROVERBS 3:6–8)

It is humbling and a bit awkward to seek His will in all we do, but it is far too costly to neglect His counsel. Sometimes we are tempted to run ahead, saying, "Hey, God, I have got this one covered. I have been here before so I won't trouble Your throne with this. I'll just proceed how I think best." Wrong! You are headed for a mess. Instead of being foolish and arrogant we are admonished to "fear the LORD and turn away from evil." We fear the Lord when we depart from evil and tremble at God's holy Word.

Being true is also tied to trust, for you can trust the truthful. I have friends who speak the truth to me. I can trust them because I have never known them to be false or deceitful with me. They are not perfect, but they have been tried and found true. They do not always say what I want to hear but they faithfully speak what I need to hear. They even are faithful to speak truth when they know I am not ready to listen—they still put it out there so when I am ready, their counsel will call me back to reason. I can trust them because they are not only honest with me . . . they are honest with themselves.

God cannot resist daughters who trust Him with all their hearts.

In these days where nurture is so desperately needed, we need a host of women who walk honestly with others as well as with themselves. In the next chapter, we will review the gift of intuition and how we can nurture the inner voice that is too often suppressed.

6

Intuition

The only real valuable thing is intuition.
—ALBERT EINSTEIN

Women are by nature intuitive, but too frequently the power of this gift is lost. In this chapter we are going to review at length why we need to recover this awareness.

Listen to the words of world changer Golda Meir: "Trust yourself. Create the kind of self that you will be happy to live with all your life. Make the most of yourself by fanning the tiny, inner sparks of possibility into flames of achievement." To fan the inner sparks of inspiration into flame, we need the guidance of intuition. God is challenging us to release the light and life that have been quickened within each of us. Some of us have quenched the light of our God-given feminine intuition and it needs to be reignited.

For example, has there ever been a time when you saw something other than the obvious, but you reasoned your initial perception away only to discover later you were correct?

As a woman, you have probably experienced the nagging sense that all is not well, not without, but within. Perhaps it comes in the form of a deep, unsettling feeling often referred to as woman's intuition.

Years ago I read some research on the prevention of children abductions. The author said that very often children were abducted or molested by people the mothers never felt comfortable with. They would wrestle with these feelings and even give voice to them, but their input was disregarded. The author's advice to mothers: trust that inward warning.

I had this inner warning play out in a bit different way. In the final month of my pregnancy with my fourth son, Arden, I lay awake an entire night with a nagging feeling all was not well. I was four days past my due date, large and uncomfortable, but it was more than that. I was awakened by a sudden violent movement. There was only one, then he was still. Instinctively I cradled my large belly and spoke soothing words to comfort him.

But I knew something was amiss. My sense of alarm was so real I considered driving myself immediately to the hospital to have the baby checked out. I waited in the dark to see if the movement would happen again. Nothing more occurred, but I still could not shake my concern. When John woke at six o'clock, he found his pregnant wife dressed and ready to go. I was at the doctor's office as soon as their doors opened so they could check the baby's heart rate.

It was normal and he was in good position John was relieved, but I was not. My doctor sensed my angst.

"Lisa, you are the boss here. I have never had a baby. This is your fourth, and if you feel something is not right, I will listen to you."

Right then and there my doctor empowered me to listen to my body and my intuition. "This baby needs to be born," I said. In response my doctor set everything into motion and in the process more than likely saved my son's life. We discovered later that the cord was wrapped twice tightly around his neck. What if the doctor had discounted my foreboding? What if I had been afraid of looking foolish or pushy? My beautiful son Arden might not be with us.

Pay Attention

But I believe intuition is even more than a warning signal. It is our truest sense of self, which perceives when others are false or untrue. You see a smile, a hug, a handshake, but you sense there is no genuine warmth behind them. You listen to what you want to believe is truth, yet all the while you know a lie is hiding within. Something is amiss—there's an intangible disconnect that you cannot place a tangible finger on.

I am not referring to intuition's counterpart, suspicion (more on this one later), which tends to expect the worst, but to a sort of enlightenment accompanied by a sense of surprise. You are actually caught off guard and a bit perturbed by what you sense or discern in an encounter.

As a woman in a world of changing perspectives, I never want to cause problems. (Remember, women are answers, not problems!). But because I was afraid of causing trouble, like many other women, I have pushed down those warning sensations when they arose. Other times I just plain reasoned them away. Perhaps you have done the same. I denied what I sensed and distrusted my initial perceptions. I scolded myself with words like, *Why can't you let it go? Don't be so negative or critical! They probably didn't mean it that way. You are just imagining things.*

But more often than not, time has proven the things I saw when I wasn't looking…were accurate. This initial innocence of perspective is key because suspicion frequently, mistakenly perceives what it is looking for.

I remember distinct phrases, facial expressions, and snippets of dialogues or first impressions from years past. There were interchanges with others when looks and innuendos weighted an encounter with secondary meanings.

> *Intuition is a spiritual faculty and does not explain, but simply points the way.*
> —Florence Scovel Shinn

John and I sometimes walk away from a conversation and I check in with him: "Did you hear that? What do you think they meant by that?" Sometimes John would have noticed the same thing, but often he did not even remember it until I brought it back to his attention. "Yes, now you mention it, Lisa, that was a bit odd." Over the years we have learned to trust one another in this area—what one misses the other often sees.

Intuition at Work

There was an incident where my husband requested a meeting with a number of leaders, and I was the only female present. I came at my husband's invitation because the subject matter very much affected both of us. In those types of situations, John values my immediate involvement and input because far too much is lost in translation—I want details and nuances but John brings me only headlines.

Even though John had alerted the group that I would be a part of the discussion, my presence was less than welcomed by the group's leader. Actually, even before the meeting began, the host pastor did his best not only to disqualify my presence but to invalidate my input. I made the mistake of offering an opinion in the form of a question and he immediately pounced on it. As the meeting progressed, any discussion that involved John and me was directed singularly to John. Any question I posed was completely ignored.

A very clear signal was sent out to all those present: *Lisa may be in this room, but she will not be acknowledged*. I was afraid to open my mouth, so I just watched and listened. John tried to include me several times, but I was just not going to jump into the mix again.

After the meeting, one of the young men pulled me aside and offered a word of comfort. "I was thinking the same thing you said—you just beat me to it." *Yes, silly me,* I thought. *I should have known to be quiet*. Then another leader who was present offered further insight: "He just doesn't like processing things with women." Okay, so what do you say to that? "I'm sorry for being female"?

> ### I would rather trust a woman's instinct than a man's reason.
> —STANLEY BALDWIN

John was uncomfortable with what had transpired as well, but I wanted to avoid any further conflict. I did not want to cause a breach or disconnect between John and the leader just because he did not want to connect with me. John raised his concerns on our drive home, but I just echoed the input of the associate and shrugged my shoulders, saying, "It's okay. He just doesn't process things with women...but I am glad you do."

I stuffed it and doubted the validity of any contribution I might make. My presence was unnecessary. I hadn't added anything of value to that meeting. I had created tension merely by sitting there because I was female. I decided then and there that

John should go to future meetings alone. I was just a hindrance to the process.

Needless to say, when John tried to include me in the next meeting I found a way to excuse myself. Even though I was not willing to pursue the issue further, the meeting had set off an alarm within my spirit that just would not go away. Time passed and I began to revisit the incident in my mind as I heard other women speak of similar experiences with this leader. These women knew nothing of my encounter.

I began to wonder why this man viewed what God called a "good" addition to the world of men (women) as a hindrance and their contribution unnecessary? God was the one who said it was not good for men to do life without the voices of women! Time marched on and it was discovered that he was conflicted in his own life. For some reason this caused him to limit the input of women in his world.

It's Not Personal

> ### *No problem can be solved on the same level at which you meet it.*
> —ALBERT EINSTEIN

I cannot think of anyone who could have stated this principle with more clarity or authority. Einstein was an utterly brilliant physicist and a logics genius, but for all his mastery of numbers he was the most powerful in his approach to theories. He dared to look at the elements of this world differently; as a physicist he understood the frailty of time and how the natural appearances of things could be very limited.

In my conflict with that pastor, I could have attempted to solve the problem on the level where I'd met it. I could have railroaded the issue, forced my involvement (after all, John invited me), and demanded equal treatment and input. I could have corrected the asides and exercised my God-given right to be included. But the truth is...I was never really the issue.

If I made the conflict personal, there would be no true or lasting solution. This problem was not going to be solved around the table where I had met it—it ran so much deeper than I knew that day. The day I heard the news of this leader's troubled life, I fought believing it. It couldn't be true! How did I miss it? Then I heard the Holy Spirit gently whisper and instruct me, "It is true, Lisa, and now you will understand a lot of things and you will know it was never about you."

> ### *If I made the conflict personal, there would be no true or lasting solution.*

I have wasted far too much time, thought, and energy trying to make sense of the senseless...and so have you. Each of us must decide those days are over. Daughters, you will come up against many problems and conflicts. You may be tempted to take many of them personally. I implore you, fight this temptation. These issues and asides will never be successfully navigated from a personal perspective, so don't make it personal. Why? Because, please understand, this was *never* truly about you.

Your parents' divorce was never about you. The people who abused or used you—it was never about you. The friend who betrayed you—it was never truly about you. It would not have been different if you had been a "good girl." You didn't ask to be molested, raped, or abandoned. You did not deserve what was done to you. It is time to rise out of the dust of earthbound reasoning. Forgive and move on, but stop exhausting yourself trying to make sense out of the senseless.

If you don't believe me, then pause and look at this from

another vantage point. Remember, if you will, a time when you were cruel or unkind to others. Was it truly all about them or was it really your own anger, pain, or unresolved issues lashing out? Did you put down others to make yourself look strong? Did you hurt because you were hurting? Was it really about them?

The Battle Is Spiritual

As humans, we almost always are introduced to our problems in the realm of the physical or emotional, but this first clash does not yield the insight and perspective necessary to format any viable solution. To gain this perspective we must delve a bit deeper, or, as C. S. Lewis would say, go higher up and further in.

> For *we are not fighting against flesh-and-blood enemies, but against evil rulers and authorities of the unseen world, against mighty powers in this dark world, and against evil spirits in the heavenly places.* (EPHESIANS 6:12)

The unseen, eternal realm rules the seen and temporal. The unseen enemy who wars against our soul does not want us using the eternal weapons of warfare that reach into his realm. He wants us to jostle each other and flail around with our awkward, earthbound weaponry. He wants us to fight what we can see and touch and keep our hands off his realm. He wants us to act as though we are yet citizens of this earth and forget that our citizenship is in heaven.

> We are human, but we don't wage war as humans do. We use God's mighty weapons, not worldly weapons, to knock down the strongholds of human reasoning and to destroy false arguments. (2 CORINTHIANS 10:3–4)

Here is an earthbound example to bring this home. Recently I found water pooling in our master bathroom. At first I was confused as to its source. I had not discovered it until late at night when everything was unusually quiet and I heard the dripping. Following the sound, I looked up and realized water was falling from the exhaust fan cut into the master bathroom ceiling. I was a bit disquieted that this was happening. We had never had a leak in this ceiling before! Was our house falling apart?

I called John in so he could review the situation. He informed me it was not a leak at all. The dripping water was an interior response to the outside weather conditions. He then reminded me our house was under the onslaught of 50-mph winter winds. Outside a fierce blizzard raged that had already dumped nearly two feet of snow on our doorstep. The winds were so intense the snow was traveling sideways. Our house had never before experienced such severe storm conditions. This is why a small percentage of snow had gained entrance through the venting in the roof. When the storm passed, the water no longer gained entrance.

When there is a leak, we can put bowls all over the floor to collect the drops as they fall, but if we are going to solve the real problem we have to go to the source.

*Women are God's answer to hurting relationships,
a dying world, and an impotent church.*

If you are intuitive at all, you realize that we live in a world where the conditions have changed. Catching the fallout will not bring any true, long-term resolution. God is awakening women who are in tune with the real problem or the cause (there are storms raging outside, beating against our lives and homes) and the true answers (it is not personal or with people). The enemy is operating full force and he is after our power.

Women are God's answer to hurting relationships, a dying world, and an impotent church. Women are God's beautiful problem solvers. (If you do not know this, I covered it extensively in my book *Fight Like a Girl*). Far too often we are content to manage the chess pieces on the board in front of us rather than confront the powers they represent. We must come up to higher ground if we are to gain a problem-solving perspective.

Women: Agents of Truth

There is a true King and a false one, a magnificent heaven and a terrifying hell. We presently wander a battlefield called Earth, which is caught between night and day, death and life, and what we see now will one day pass away.

You, daughter, are an agent of truth who cannot afford to distrust the light within you. Doubt is one of the mightiest weapons your enemy raises against you. It will cause you to hesitate and waiver in unbelief and fear. Press in and get the counsel of heaven.

If you need wisdom, ask our generous God, and he will give it to you. He will not rebuke you for asking. But when you ask him, be sure that your faith is in God alone. Do not waver, for a person with divided loyalty is as unsettled as a wave of the sea that is blown and tossed by the wind.

(JAMES 1:5–6)

There are some powerful insights here we need to settle in our spirits if we are going to be women who are forces to be reckoned with. First, if you need wisdom, ask God. Second, settle that He is happy to advise you. Next, enter into an expectant mind-set: you have asked . . . He will answer. This means you watch and listen for His response.

> *Reality is merely an illusion,*
> *albeit a very persistent one.*
>
> —ALBERT EINSTEIN

When I first became a Christian, I was really troubled by this verse in James—it actually made me a bit afraid to ask for wisdom. I mean, what if I asked but wasn't really expecting an answer? Or what if I doubted that God heard? Then there was the doubting I expressed when He spoke: "God, are You sure? I will just ask again just in case I heard wrong."

Sometimes I'd say to my husband, "John, I think we need to pray again."

John would get so frustrated with me. "Lisa, you are being double-minded."

I would correct him: "No, John, actually it is quite possible I am triple-minded on this one! I am more confused than you will even know."

I would sit in the middle of the floor, Bible open, waiting for some audible voice from heaven. I would listen for verses, page numbers, even the name of one of the biblical books would be helpful. Sometimes there would be nothing. Not easily deterred, I would add in a hunger strike: "I just won't eat until I get the answer."

But you are probably smarter than I am and already understand what it took me years to learn: God answers in His own timing and manner. The trick is walking away from your time of prayer believing the answer is yours when in that moment you did not hear a thing.

Daughters, believe you have your answer and soon you will know your answer. Once you've asked, in the Spirit it is done.

To walk in intuition, you must believe God has set you on this earth as an answer. Develop the mind-set *I am an answer, not a problem!* You cannot be true to yourself without a measure of intuition, so let's look more closely at this priceless commodity. Here again is the definition:

> INTUITION (noun): The state of being aware of or knowing something without having to discover or perceive it, or the ability to do this 2. Something known or believed instinctively, without actual evidence for it 3. Immediate knowledge of something.[1]

The definitions of intuition and intuitive carry with them the designation of an immediate sense of understanding. When the answer is presented, it is known and therefore immediately recognized. An undeniable quickening occurs when truth is heard. The Latin breakdown of *intuition* (*in* and *tueor*) yields "inward tutor,"[2] which is perfectly confirmed by Scripture:

> *But you have received the Holy Spirit, and he lives within you, so you don't need anyone to teach you what is true. For the Spirit teaches you everything you need to know, and what he teaches is true all things, and what he teaches is true—it is not a lie. So just as he has taught you, remain in fellowship with Christ.*
> (1 JOHN 2:27)

When truth is spoken the inward tutor, or the Holy Spirit of God, confirms it to you and in you. There is a distinct prompting and a release of life. You will feel a resounding "Yes, listen and receive this" inside of you. You will feel as though light and strength, truth and freedom are being poured out upon you. This will happen even if the message is one that brings correction. You will witness inwardly that it is true and the illumination will bring with it the power to embrace the cleansing, correction, or admonition. This can happen as you read, worship, pray, hear a sermon, drive your car, take a shower, or speak with a close friend.

> *But when the Father sends the Advocate as my representative—that is, the Holy Spirit—he will teach you everything and will remind you of everything I have told you. I am leaving you with a gift—peace of mind and heart. And the peace I give is a gift the world cannot give. So don't be troubled or afraid.* (JOHN 14:26–27)

The "gift" is not the Holy Spirit—He is our counselor. The gift is peace of mind and a tender new heart. Jesus gave this invaluable gift to each of us who have been reborn. The peace He gives abides even in the midst of turmoil and raging storms. There may be a few drops that remind you what is coming against you, but you are safe from the deluge that would seek to overwhelm you.

I can't even count the number of times John and I have looked at each other and said, "This is a mess. We should be panicking! So why do we have such peace?" Because this beautiful new gifted heart carries with it an unfathomable peace that surpasses our natural ability to understand. The world does not have this peace, so it often freaks when we remain calm. This is one of the many reasons it is so important that we guard our hearts, to keep them clear and clean, and protect our minds, so they may remain at rest.

New Hearts, Fresh Peace

And I will give you a new heart, and I will put a new spirit in you. I will take out your stony, stubborn heart and give you a tender, responsive heart. And I will put my Spirit in you so that you will follow my decrees and be careful to obey my regulations. (EZEKIEL 36:26–27)

God has promised us new hearts filled with healthy desires and new spirits that are obedient. It is like my new computer. When it came, it was fully loaded and free of viruses as long as I did not put any contaminated data into its system.

We have been reborn, but sometimes we need to be renewed.

Sadly, religion and wounds can muddle these new hearts and then we find them in need of healing so they can be made whole and healthy again. We have been reborn, but sometimes we needed to be renewed.

Put on your new nature, and be renewed as you learn to know your Creator and become like him. (COLOSSIANS 3:10)

How is it renewed? As we learn more of Christ, we partake of more of His nature. As I read the Bible, I feel washed and strengthened. As I worship, I feel enveloped. As I pray, I feel heard and sometimes this is all the renewal I need.

How to Get Intuition Back

In light of all this, how do we recover lost intuition or strengthen waning discernment? I think the first step is to acknowledge who is our ultimate connection with intuition and discernment.

He uncovers mysteries hidden in darkness; he brings light to the deepest gloom. He builds up nations, and he destroys them. He expands nations, and he abandons them. He strips kings of understanding and leaves them wandering in a pathless wasteland. They grope in the darkness without a light. He makes them stagger like drunkards. (Job 12:22–25)

God is the source of all intuition, discernment, and understanding. He gives it and He can take it away. This is not about an exercise of human self-actualization, but a connection with the divine and holy One. A fraction of the enlightenment of heaven is shed abroad in our earthen vessels by the power of the Holy Spirit when we become daughters of heaven. If our vision has become a bit obscured or if our discernment is a bit mired, it is up to us to take off the baskets that are far too often plopped firmly on top of us. Again, what is our purpose as God's daughters?

To give light to those who sit in darkness and in the shadow of death, and to guide us to the path of peace. (Luke 1:79)

To give light we must walk in light and steward truth well, but truth without inner peace does not work. Peace fosters an atmosphere for discernment to flourish and this insight is invaluable to the child of God: it is the ability to perceive the difference between two things, for example, between good and evil. Intuition creates a level of awareness and discernment that equips you to make a wise decision. The Word of God is the ultimate discerner of thoughts and intent, so without it we cannot really walk in truth and be wisely discerning.

The Word of God is the ultimate discerner of thoughts and intent.

Conscience at Work

To further investigate, let's examine a few more terms.

> CONSCIENCE (noun): 1. The internal sense of what is right and wrong that governs somebody's thoughts and actions, urging him or her to do the right thing.

Remember Pinocchio? He was a wooden puppet that had been quickened to animation by a fairy, but to begin with he was not really alive. He was given the opportunity to earn the privilege to be truly alive and an authentic living son to his father. This transformation from puppet to real boy would happen as he navigated life by listening to his companion, conscience.

Because Pinocchio was merely animated and not human, he lacked a real conscience and without it he was never going to become a real boy. The good fairy assigned Jiminy Cricket the task of being both his companion and moral guide. Jiminy would travel with him and act as an external voice of reason.

This proved to be a bit of a problem, though, because a cricket is rather small and not very loud (unless, of course, he is in your head). Without the advantage of an inward leading, the cricket's voice was often not strong enough to compete with the other voices that surrounded Pinocchio.

Pinocchio began with high hopes and every intention of listening to Jiminy Cricket, but was swayed the very first day before he even reached the school building. He was so completely void of discernment everything he heard sounded like a great idea. With each foolish choice, Pinocchio found himself deeper in danger and further separated from the voice of his conscience.

I am thankful our human conscience is not a small voice whispered without but a still, quiet one within. It cannot fall off our shoulders and we cannot outrun it, but we can lose touch with its frequency. It is imperative each of us tunes into our conscience with a greater accuracy than ever before. I don't know about you, but my conscience is currently pricking me for things it did not seem to mind last year. There is a greater call to be true of heart and pure in spirit as God is purging both His house and people.

We are not animals, we are humans created in the image of God. We have an inward witness of right and wrong even before we are born again. It is actually what convicts us of sin.

For example, I love my dog, she is cute, but I fear she has no conscience. She is driven by consequences, not an innate sense of right and wrong. Her conscience is not pricked as she eats my sons' Reese's peanut butter cups. She is not aware she is stealing…she is living large and in the moment. It is not until she is discovered that she feels any remorse, but please understand, I doubt she regrets eating the candy; she regrets getting caught. Our human conscience is what pricks us even before we are caught and prompts us to make it right.

According to my trusty Bible dictionary, the conscience is

> that faculty of the mind, or inborn sense of right and wrong, by which we judge of the moral character of human conduct. It is common to all men.
>
> Like all our other faculties, it has been perverted by the Fall (John 16:2; Acts 26:9; Rom. 2:15). It is spoken of as "defiled" (Titus 1:15), and "seared" (1 Tim. 4:2). A "conscience void of offence" is to be sought and cultivated (Acts 24:16; Rom. 9:1; 2 Cor. 1:12; 1 Tim. 1:5, 19; 1 Pet. 3:21).[3]

The word *conscience* (Greek: *syneidēsis*)[4] occurs some twenty-seven times in the New Testament; as just mentioned, the writers speak of a variety of conscience conditions: good, clear, weak, wounded, seared, defiled, imperfect, pure, and evil.

The Heart: Source of All Things

HEART (noun): The heart is the centre not only of spiritual activity, but of all the operations of human life.[5]

The New Testament identifies a wide assortment of heart conditions. For example, it speaks of hearts that are pure, dull, good, evil, hard, and distant from God, doubting, honest, and so forth.

The Bible teaches that there is the cleansing of the heart/conscience from the guilt of sins committed and the defilement of sin acquired. While the New Testament has a great deal to say on this subject, I want to examine one text in particular. Hebrews 10:22 draws a connection between conscience and cleansing the heart:

Let us draw near with a true heart in full assurance of faith, with our hearts sprinkled clean from an evil conscience and our bodies washed with pure water. (NKJV)

Again we have a reference to a true rather than a false heart. Next we see we must approach God with a full assurance of faith that He in fact hears us. Hearts are sprinkled clean by the blood of Jesus Christ, the spotless Lamb. Our actions are to be purged of any defilement by the washing of the water of the Word of God. When we draw near to God, we should incorporate these four things:

1. A heart that is true to itself and to others.
2. A confident assurance that God welcomes us into His presence and longs to impart His wisdom to us.

3. A clean conscience that accurately discerns between right and wrong.
4. A body cleansed of sin.

Suspicion

We have touched on this fallen form of intuition very briefly. For most of us, being suspicious comes more naturally than being intuitive or discerning. Suspicion is inbred into our culture and it is part of the old person we take off when we put on Christ.

I want you to be wise in doing right and to stay innocent of any wrong. (ROMANS 16:19)

We are instructed to be wise or well-skilled with what is good and untainted by what is evil. Far too often I have been naive and unaware of what is good and brilliant and focused instead on what is wrong. For example, I could quickly rehearse the faults of others but was less intimately acquainted with their strengths.

> **Far too often I have been naive and unaware of what is good and brilliant and focused instead on what is wrong.**

One night I just sat in my room and wept. "God, I don't want to be right about what is wrong. I want to be right about what is right!" My home church had gone through some major shaking and I was feeling overwhelmed by the confirmation of so many bad reports and suspicions. I had to close my ears to the negative and focus again on what was pure and true. In order to be wise about something you must be well acquainted

with it. You tend to live what you know, so it is far more benefi-
cial to be knowledgeable and intimately acquainted with good.
This involves surrounding your life with other men and women
who are skilled at noticing what is good in others, good in the
church, and good in our lives and world.

I am not suggesting we live in denial and never address issues or sin, but we need to address them from the perspective of
finding a solution. In our present world, everyone is an expert
in what is wrong, but where are the experts in what is right,
just, and pure? To counteract a critical and suspicious mind-
set, we must meditate on what is good.

> *Fix your thoughts on what is true, and honorable, and right,*
> *and pure, and lovely, and admirable. Think about things that*
> *are excellent and worthy of praise. Keep putting into prac-*
> *tice all you learned and received from me—everything you*
> *heard from me and saw me doing. Then the God of peace*
> *will be with you.* (PHILIPPIANS 4:8–9)

You can control what you think about, and then what you
meditate on will begin to steer what you do. I have learned I
can't let my mind run wild. If I don't keep it in check, it would
go out of control and renegade. I have to choose to think about
the lovely, admirable, honorable, and just. If I don't, my mind
will jet in the other direction. I am a positive person but my
mind can flip everything to the negative rather quickly if I have
not "fixed" my thoughts.

Notice you alone have the power to "fix" your thoughts.
My husband, pastor, or friends cannot do this thought-fixing
for me. I am the one responsible for setting the parameters and
direction of my thought life.

Suspicion is accompanied by fear and worry while true
discernment is accompanied by peace and love. Suspicion is

an unsubstantiated belief accompanied by feelings of distrust and doubt. It will tend to disbelieve what it sees. In all honesty, we will be suspicious of others when we are untrue with ourselves. After all, if you can't trust yourself, you will never trust others. There will always be a hint or shadow that blurs the true image or scenario. Suspicion is the offspring or companion of jealousy. In defining the word, Webster's dictionary included an interesting quote: "Suspicions among thoughts, are like bats among birds; they ever fly by twilight."[6]

> *Suspicion is accompanied by fear and worry while true discernment is accompanied by peace and love.*

What a telling illustration. We can gauge our thoughts to see if we are truly thinking with discernment or suspicion by the realm our thoughts inhabit. Is it shadow or light? Are we moving toward darkness in our assumptions or toward illumination? Most who wrestle with suspicion have been, at some time, sorely disappointed or ill-used. They are afraid to process things in the light because they have known so much darkness. They are afraid to let go of control of the situation and trust God for His counsel, but, beautiful one, this is what must happen. You were never meant for darkness and fear, you were created for light and love.

> *Don't worry about anything; instead, pray about everything. Tell God what you need, and thank him for all he has done. Then you will experience God's peace, which exceeds anything we can understand. His peace will guard your hearts and minds as you live in Christ Jesus.* (PHILIPPIANS 4:6–7)

The suspicious often want plans figured out ahead of time. They do not want any unwelcome twists, turns, or surprises. They want to be assured they are safe and in control. Often suspicious people would rather be right about others being wrong than to be caught off guard. Those who expect the worst of others are rarely disappointed.

Suspicion will not lead you to safety, it will lead you to a place of deception. You will think you are right as you watch others being proved wrong, but this has never been the calling of the daughters of God. We are called to a higher purpose and perspective. We are those who turn the wrongs to right, those who build, not those who tear down.

> *But the wisdom from above is first of all pure. It also peace loving, gentle at all times, and willing to yield to others. It is full of mercy and good deeds. It shows no favoritism and is always sincere. And those who are peacemakers will plant seeds of peace and reap a harvest of righteousness.*
>
> (JAMES 3:17–18)

We can judge where our wisdom is coming from by what accompanies it. Those using the discernment and wisdom of heaven do not have to prove themselves right. They stay true to their convictions without forcing others to agree, because they understand that in the end, truth and goodness will prevail.

On the other hand, suspicious people will always pressure you to pass judgment on others, to side with their counsel, while discernment is content to wait.

> *Don't let evil conquer you, but conquer evil by doing good.*
>
> (ROMANS 12:21)

Check yourself:

Have you been true to yourself?
Do you remember a time when your intuition was accurate?
Do you recall a time you suppressed it and were sorry?
Why were you afraid to give it expression?
Have you been more excellent and accurate about what is wrong or with what is right in your [workplace, marriage, friendships, church, children]?
Which has a stronger pull on your life—suspicion or intuition?

Let's pray.

Heavenly Father, I want to be excellent with what is good and innocent of what is evil. Forgive me the times I have suppressed my intuition and been untrue to my heart or self. Forgive me for the times this violation of self has caused me to be false with others. Wash me clean and separate the precious from the vile, that my heart would be a wellspring of life and refreshing. Renew my heart and sensitize my soul to the voice of Your Holy Spirit.

7

Mentor or Mother

Looking back, I find it almost comical. My assistant, Judy, called my cell phone and caught me shopping for groceries at the local health food store.

"Lisa, you just got the most exciting invitation!"

"What is it?" I asked as I slowed my cart to a halt in the cereal aisle.

"You've been invited to speak at a mentoring conference!" she responded enthusiastically.

My pause surprised her. "You're going to accept it, aren't you?"

"When is it?" I hedged.

"April of next year."

"Who are the other speakers?"

Judy reeled off an impressive list of names.

"Let me pray about it."

"Sure. I thought you would be excited—it seems such a good fit for you," Judy said.

I just wasn't sure, though. It seemed like a good fit for all the other speakers, but not for me. I was afraid I wouldn't have what was needed. Disregarding my fears, I accepted the invitation hoping between my acceptance and the occurrence of the actual event, I would somehow morph into a better fit.

Time flew by and when April came, it found me home nursing a broken nose. I broke it surfing in Hawaii and unfortunately waited two weeks before I even went to the doctor's office. But when the initial swelling hadn't decreased and my ears still wouldn't clear on the airplanes, I had to come to terms with the truth: I had blocked air passages. The kind doctor explained my options. Either I could have immediate surgery to reopen these air passages, or I could wait three months and he could rebreak it, then set it. Not willing to experience a voluntary break, I signed up for surgery the very next day. I would have the nose I'd now broken twice, reset.

On Easter Sunday I was home with a splint glued to my face. John refused my appeals to go to church. "Lisa, we are not in a position to explain to everyone what happened, and I am not going to have people think I punched you! Just stay home and get ready for your meeting next week."

After waving good-bye to my handsome family of five men, I climbed back into bed, a bit dejected, with my laptop and Bible. I did a few word searches on the topic of mentoring and finally expressed my true fear and frustration to the Father: "What am I doing speaking at a mentoring conference?" I felt more like the poster child of how *not* to do things rather than an example for others to follow.

> ### *I felt more like the poster child of how* not *to do things than an example for others to follow.*

I thought of the other speakers. They were women with a Christian heritage, and most of them could even sing. I wouldn't have been surprised if they all could trace their Christian lineage back to the Ark.

And then there was me...first-generation Christian, former heathen. While these women had been praying for godly husbands, I was involved in full-fledged tryouts for my college's sexual gymnastics team. Even after I was saved, sanctified, and married, I had been known to throw things at my husband and yell at my children!

I imagined beginning my session with this introduction: "Hi, I am Lisa, and I have been asked here today to provide an example of what you should not do!" I pictured women getting up and leaving as they mumbled to themselves, "Who needs to hear that? We want someone who knows what she is talking about!"

My imaginings were growing way too vivid, so I prayed. "Father, what portion could I possibly bring to this table? Your daughters are coming to hear from a mentor. What should I share with them? They need to be mentored, so they can in turn mentor others....Help me."

I am not looking for mentors...
I am looking for mothers.

I was whining, and I knew it. I really did not expect any type of answer, but one came anyway: "Tell My daughters I am looking for something more. I am not looking for mentors...I am looking for mothers."

Mothers! A mother I could be, for a mother I was, but what was so special about a mother? Probably most of the women there were mothers and some grandmothers. After all, didn't we need mentors because our mothers could take us only so far?

God clarified what at first was slightly confusing. "Mentors tend to reproduce themselves, but mothers want more for their sons and daughters than they ever had themselves." Then the comparisons came as fast as I could record them. I thanked God for the invite because it opened up my mind to a whole new way of thinking.

The Difference Defined

To gain a better understanding, let's define the word *mentor*.

> MENTOR (noun): 1. A wise and trusted counselor or teacher. 2. Mentor Greek Mythology. Odysseus's trusted counselor, in whose guise Athena became the guardian and teacher of Telemachus.[1]

In Homer's *Odyssey*, Mentor was the friend Odysseus left in charge of his household. He acted as both teacher and protector of the son in Odysseus's absence. The original mentor was named Mentor, and he was actually put in place to steward what Odysseus already possessed. Mentor was more of a maintainer or guardian in the father's absence. He did not have the power to take the son any higher than himself.

In our present culture, more often than not, *mentor* is a professional term used to describe a guide or counselor. Mentoring is entrusted to skilled professionals. But mothering is not professional, it is just messy. Mentors earn the right to be trusted through accomplishment; mothers are entrusted with the precious by way of personal sacrifice, whether they have earned the right or not...which makes it all a bit dicey.

Mentoring is often assigned a time slot or scheduled on a regular basis—mothering is not. For mothers, the greatest needs are simultaneously extremely urgent and exceptionally inconvenient (think of sick children throwing up in the middle of the night). Mentoring might be orderly and accompanied by a syllabus, but mothering comes without a manual. It is a willingness to lead and train others as you venture into various realms and seasons of life. They see the good, the bad, and the ugly. (At least my kids have.)

Mentors encourage others to follow their lead by way of their example, but mothers don't necessarily want their daughters to always look and act like them. With each of my children I prayed for a new and vastly improved version of myself. Often a mother's greatest contribution comes when she lays down her life to bring forth life. There is a single event called labor, but childbirth happens every day, and it is usually not until the child grows that he or she learns of physical sacrifices his or her mother made. What daughter hasn't gained a greater appreciation for her mother after undergoing her own first labor?

Before you draw the conclusion I think mentoring is wrong or even shallow, allow me to clarify myself. I don't think for a moment mentoring is bad. It's a place for women to start connecting. I am just not sure it will be enough. Naomi did not mentor Ruth—she mothered her. Paul did not mentor Timothy—he fathered him. Elizabeth did not merely instruct Mary, she blessed her as a mother would.

Motherhood: Its Depths and History

Jobs come and go, but once you are a mother there is a connection for life. After you have experienced the blessing of motherhood, you can never quite look at a baby, a child, or even a teen the same way. This connection begins with the quickening of life within. This awakening can happen when you feel the first flutter in your womb, or when you receive your long-awaited child through adoption. Whether you gave physical birth, or selflessly cared for a child another birthed but could not care for, the motherly bond is made. Once the spirit of adoption has been ignited, there is really no turning back.

It will be like a woman suffering the pains of labor. When her child is born, her anguish gives way to joy because she has brought a new baby into the world. (JOHN 16:21)

I used to think John 16:21 might have been the only wrong Scripture in the Bible. Six months after I had my first child I still remembered the pain—acutely! The memory was so vivid that I was actually afraid to have another child. I went to a lot of trouble trying to figure out the dynamics of pain avoidance. When I went into labor with my second son, Austin, I kept thinking, *Something must be wrong with me, because I am remembering all this!* Jesus was not saying women would blank out and totally lose recall, but that the joy they experienced at birth would displace the anguish experienced in labor.

Why is the pain swallowed up in joy? After the Fall, life came forth out of the pain. How many of you have experienced anguish in your life? Well, a mother knows how to turn anguish into joy. Are you glimpsing why mothers are so crucial to our world, and do you see why the enemy has worked overtime to try to remove them or reduce their role?

A mother knows how to turn anguish into joy.

Decades ago, women rejected the image of the passive, quiet, stay-at-home mother. For various reasons, women felt they could never fulfill such expectations. The images presented to us back then, June Cleaver and Donna Reed, seemed surreal and incongruous with their hopes and dreams. As time passed, women began to wonder if staying at home as mother was really fulfilling—and sometimes, even safe. They seemed so vulnerable and isolated with domestic violence and divorce on the rise.

Then housewives began to look away from traditional roles to find satisfaction and safety. This required a much more male approach, so women merged mothering with the pursuit of professions. Women ventured out into the workforce, trying to survive. Far too often in the process, we lost part of God's purpose for our lives.

In an attempt to be true to ourselves, we forgot the truth that in life *we are not what we do, we are what we pass on.* Selfishly we tried to protect our personhood and lost many things that make this life worth living. I do not believe any TV icon has captured the true, strong, deep essence of being a mother. It would not have been possible for a sitcom to capture something so intimate and wide in its range and transcendent in its scale.

Perhaps the old stereotypes must go away so the new images can be brought forth. Perhaps only then will we appreciate the uniqueness of our gifts and the power of mothers' influence. Neither the gift of a mother or the power of her nurture could flourish in a culture that valued self-preservation above life or family. This is the case whether you work or stay home.

Wisdom Awaits Us

So where are the mothers for our generation? If you look closely, you will find glimpses of these mothers everywhere. Amazingly, you will find them in all age ranges as well. They are often waiting to be called upon. You will find them in homes, hosting television programs, writing articles and books, running successful corporations, holding government positions, teaching children, and administering health care. These are merely the jobs they do, but even in these positions I believe they hunger for more. They listen, awaiting the stirring of God's Spirit.

What we look for will not come from resurrecting a surreal domestic image. The daughters of our time are not interested in watching us as we pretend to be perfect. Every human alive has made acquaintance with failure. These daughters look for something a bit more intimate than perfection. They want to know what we learned when we failed. They hope we will be brave enough to be honest, authentic, and wise with our words and life lessons. They hope we will strain the bitterness from our stories and present them as wine, laced with promise.

Wisdom has built her house; she has carved its seven columns. She has prepared a great banquet, mixed her wines, and set the table. (PROVERBS 9:1–2)

The banquet we prepare in this life will either sustain or weaken those who attend. The foods we partake of will either strengthen or destroy us. The homes in which we serve this feast will be built by either the strength of wisdom or by the slight and cunning of our hands. Will our supporting structures be upheld by the strength of sturdy, carved pillars or flimsy, superficial props?

What we do not accomplish in our lifetimes we will leave for another generation to resolve. What we do not model for them now, they will have to learn later. There have been many years of waste and foolishness, and yet I still hear the voice of wisdom calling the mothers and drawing the daughters to herself.

Come, eat my food and drink the wine I have mixed. Leave your simple ways behind, and begin to live; learn to use good judgment. (PROVERBS 9:5–6)

Do you hear her voice, the voice of wisdom? It is there if you will choose to listen. In the busy streets she cries out to us, but you must know what her voice sounds like in order to hear her above the cultural noise, to hear her above the din.

I remember when I first cried out for her voice, her food, and her drink. I remember distinctly wanting wisdom to be my sustenance. I was new to Christianity, in my earlier twenties, and a promotional representative for a major cosmetic company. I traveled to eight states regularly, leaving on Monday mornings and returning on Friday afternoons. This meant I spent quite a few nights in hotel rooms. Each night I would retreat to my room, order room service, take a bath, and devour my Bible for hours. I rarely turned on the TV on those evenings. I sat in a bed with a notepad. I sat many nights alone in my room, crying out in desperation, "Wisdom, I need you! I cry out for you! I call you my sister!" I modeled my prayer literally after the Proverbs admonition.

Say to wisdom, "You are my sister," and call understanding
your nearest kin. (PROVERBS 7:4 NKJV)

Now it seems almost silly, but I truly did not know what else to do. I so wanted to attend the feast, but was afraid I would not find my way there. God was faithful to impart the strength of wisdom. As I studied His Word, I found her. I am concerned too many daughters learn in loneliness what they could learn more rapidly from those who have gone before them. For them, this banquet of refreshing just does not happen. Bitter waters spill forth from bitter lives and threaten to pollute the water and wine of the daughters. Sadly, women are more likely to pass on their pain and anguish than the promise and joy that come with birthing life.

Sadly, women are more likely to pass on
their pain and anguish than the promise
and joy that come with birthing life.

We Choose What We Pass On

Divorce has given birth to bitter phrases like, "Your father..."
The devastating rip in a family declares the mother's distance
and rejects her offspring as aligned with an enemy. Both dynamics effectively poison a young daughter's heart with the
burden of choosing whom to love and whom to hate.

*Good people leave an inheritance to their grandchildren, but
the sinner's wealth passes to the godly.* (PROVERBS 13:22)

Money should follow the good and the godly. Our wealth
should travel with the next generations and grow in strength
with each hand it passes through. Let me clarify, however,
wealth is not found only in money. Proverbs isn't restricting inheritance to monetary gifts. The point is, whether it is money,
wisdom, knowledge, or walking in the fear of the Lord, our
children need us to pass on a blessing to them. Wealth was never
meant to be something each child and grandchild struggled to
establish. They were meant to inherit something from their
parents. But in today's culture, more often than not, children
do not inherit what they need—financially, emotionally, and
spiritually—to make it. They inherit regret, pain, and mistakes
instead.

How many inheritances have been utterly lost because of
the emotional, spiritual, and financial betrayal of divorce? How
many generations of men and women have labored long and
hard, only to watch their relational riches slip away from them?
Without the establishment of strong and healthy relationships,
money means nothing. Sadly, many grandparents fail to leave
an inheritance for their grandchildren, whether physical or
spiritual resources. They simply have nothing left to leave.

When homes are destroyed, houses become assets to be

divided while joint bank accounts are neatly separated and drained off to pay legal fees. Even worse than financial devastation, there is the devastating loss of heritage. No hope or history is passed on to guide the ones around us.

But what if one generation of mothers said *no* to all this? What if today, godly women everywhere decided they would no longer allow fear to give intimate counsel? What if we said, "Enough with the anguish" and began to call forth life? What if we sought to give others what no one left to us?

We are the ones who choose what the next generation will inherit. Our children, whether born of the heart or of the body, will inherit one of two things: God's promises, or our fears. There is no neutral ground for any of us. Each and every generation of women is given the gift of time and influence. How will we choose to spend it on the daughters now before us?

> ### What if today, godly women everywhere decided they would no longer allow fear to give intimate counsel?

The connection happens on both sides. Daughters, you must seek out the mothers in your lives and glean all you can. You are called to so much more than most of us older generations even dared to dream of. Daughters, we have seen you only from afar but we choose to release blessings and promise into your future. Go the distance—be strong, free, and unafraid.

I believe the women of my age group have the opportunity to act as runners between the generations. It is the privilege of the middle-aged women to extend a mother's hand to the younger daughters who follow us, while at the same time we grasp hold of the older women who have forged ahead of us. In this way we act as a bridge between the age groups and link the strengths of all three.

A New Generation of Ruths

We are not unlike a generation of Ruths, who have found themselves widowed and alone while yet in our youth. Without a provider, and without the wisdom of the generations before us, we have the opportunity to go back, like Naomi's other daughter-in-law, Orpah, and seek out another husband. Or we can get what we need from a woman who has entered the next season of life. Ruth was not really interested in what Naomi could give her—Naomi had nothing left to give. Ruth was interested in what Naomi could connect her with, a living God who was visiting His people with provision after a season of famine. Naomi was returning home.

> *Naomi heard in Moab that the* Lord *had blessed his people in Judah by giving them good crops again. So Naomi and her daughters-in-law got ready to leave Moab to return to her homeland.* (Ruth 1:6)

Following Naomi did not look like the right choice or course for Ruth. Most young widows probably wouldn't think staying with their former mothers-in-law the most opportune choice. Ruth's mother-in-law was also an old widow, with little or no hope of remarrying. In addition to this, Naomi suffered the devastating loss of both of her sons, Mahlon and Chilion. Naomi tried to discourage Ruth from following her, but this daughter's heart was set.

> *But Ruth replied, "Don't ask me to leave you and turn back. Wherever you go, I will go; wherever you live, I will live. Your people will be my people, and your God will be my God."* (Ruth 1:16)

Naomi realized it was no further use to try and dissuade Ruth, so she brought her along as she returned to Bethlehem. When the women saw Naomi returning, they rushed out to greet her. But she told them,

> *Don't call me Naomi....Instead, call me Mara, for the Almighty has made life very bitter for me. I went away full, but the LORD has brought me home empty.* (RUTH 1:20–21)

Listen to how she described her life: "I went away full [a husband and two sons] but the LORD has brought me home empty [a widow with a widowed daughter-in-law]." The name *Naomi* means "my pleasantness."[2] She felt this a cruel irony and asked the women to call her Mara, which means "bitter."

I have to wonder if there is a generation of older women who are on the verge of changing their full names to empty ones. We mustn't let them! We have to seek them out and tell them we will not leave them to die bitter and exhausted of hope when God longs to restore their joy! We are their link for rejuvenation, and they are ours. You see, Ruth needed Naomi as much as Naomi needed Ruth. Naomi knew things Ruth did not and presented her with opportunities and connections she would not have had otherwise.

Ruth needed Naomi as much as Naomi needed Ruth.

Naomi was destitute, but she still had an inheritance in the land. As a mother in Israel she was allowed to glean in the fields. When God pours out His provision He wants it to encompass all who need it. Ruth begged Naomi to allow her to do the work and soon found herself in the field of Boaz, one of

Naomi's kin. When he met Ruth, he invited her to remain in his fields. There she could glean unafraid of any harassment. And then Boaz blessed Ruth, saying,

> *I also know about everything you have done for your mother-in-law since the death of your husband. I have heard how you left your father and mother and your own land to live here among complete strangers. May the LORD, the God of Israel, under whose wings you have come to take refuge, reward you fully for what you have done.* (RUTH 2:11–12)

Ruth's sacrifice had special meaning to Boaz. His mother was Rahab, the harlot who left everything to embrace God and find refuge under His wings. The first thing we find Naomi passed on to her daughter-in-law Ruth was the ability to glean in the field what the harvesters left behind. Ruth was invited to join the group of women who gleaned exclusively in Boaz's field until the end of the barley and wheat harvest. It is important to note the name. *Boaz* means "in him is strength."[3] These were the women of strength who worked diligently in his fields so nothing would be lost and all would be fed.

Where Are You, Women of Strength?

Is this not just what we are looking for today—women of strength? So many have been left behind by the harvesters because no one knew how to look for them. Gleaning is painstaking work; one has to sift through what others have cast aside. It is to snatch from decay and to see what slipped by the first pass of the harvesters.

Naomi discerned the bigger purpose in Ruth's gleaning in Boaz's field. Ruth blessed Naomi's life with food, hope, and purpose. It was time to do the same for Ruth. Naomi told Ruth to position herself for provision by going to the threshing floor, uncovering Boaz's feet, and lying down there.

Ruth blessed Naomi's life....
It was time to do the same for Ruth.

Around midnight Boaz suddenly woke up and turned over. He was surprised to find a woman lying at his feet! "Who are you?" he asked. "I am your servant Ruth," she replied. "Spread the corner of your covering over me, for you are my family redeemer." (RUTH 3:8–9)

Ruth's actions and words let Boaz know she would accept him as a husband, though he was older than she. Boaz might never have assumed this had Ruth not chosen to honor Naomi and the legacy of her family. Boaz redeemed Naomi's land and took Ruth as his wife.

And with the land I have acquired Ruth, the Moabite widow of Mahlon, to be my wife. This way she can have a son to carry on the family name of her dead husband and to inherit the family property here in his hometown. (RUTH 4:10)

Ruth and Boaz married and she conceived a son. When the baby was born, she put him in the arms of Naomi. Naomi's friends said,

Praise the Lord, who has now provided a redeemer for your family! May this child be famous in Israel. May he restore your youth and care for you in your old age. For he is the son of your daughter-in-law who loves you and has been better to you than seven sons! (RUTH 4:14–15)

Then something beautiful and amazing transpires. Naomi nurses this baby! Once again, she has a son in her arms. She has the promise of an heir in her future.

The child, Obed, joined a famous legacy. Obed was the father of Jesse and the grandfather of King David. What if Ruth had not followed Naomi? What if Naomi had changed her name and nature to Bitterness? Would King David ever have sat upon the throne? Who would have penned some of the Psalms and fathered Solomon? Who would have praised God in the wilderness and slain the giant before the armies?

Where are the Naomis who will turn their hearts toward Ruths? Where are the Ruths who will bless the Naomis? Where are the kinsmen-redeemers who will cover the women who simply want to do their part?

In the next chapter we are going to review a New Testament example of another two women who were able to capture this dynamic and translate it to a revelation of the impossible and miraculous.

8

Elizabeth and Mary

Even though we are not opening with a definition, I believe these two women of the Bible define, in part, what God is looking for today. For the past few years I have been comparing and contrasting the lives of these two pivotal women. I believe both represent more than godly historical female figures. They were powerful women who prophetically traced a path for us to contemplate and follow today. Because of this I want to take the time to delve into their lives and conversations on a bit more intimate level. I believe, hidden in their lives of obedience and sanctification, we will glimpse the beauty of present promise and discover we are not so different from these women of long ago.

These amazing women lived in a season when women had little or no voice in their community of faith, let alone the world at large. How did Elizabeth and Mary live in such a way that their private words were set before the world? What was their relationship? How did they release both prophetic praise and promise that echoes with such clarity? Their words even now reach forth through passages of time extending blessing and truth.

Somehow Mary and Elizabeth learned to steward in secret what most women of their day would have rejected outright. Let us not assume anything as we approach their lives and watch as both the impossible and miraculous are brought forth. It is important we get this dynamic because we have a desperate need for the reintroduction of both.

To have this understanding we need the benefit of perspective and a frame of reference; we need to imagine the atmosphere where all this happened. In this chapter we will wade through quite a few Scriptures. Rather than skip over these, I need you to review them with me, for it is my earnest prayer you'll receive God's living Word as your own. I believe the Spirit may show you things my eyes have missed, so open your eyes and heart to this living Word.

What Humans Do with Silence

Our story begins as the door of one dispensation closes and another opens. Like a long intermission between acts of a play, four hundred years of silence had passed between the book of Malachi and the birth of John the Baptist. Malachi closes with God's promise to send

> *The prophet Elijah....His preaching will turn the hearts of fathers to their children, and the hearts of children to their fathers.* (MALACHI 4:5–6)

These words set the stage for Matthew, Mark, Luke, and John, which speak of the birth of Christ and His forerunner, John. Let us likewise pause and ask some questions.

What does the world look like when God is quite suddenly

and completely silent? What happens to His people when four hundred years pass without direction or communication from heaven? No word. No wonder. No miraculous provision, no anointed leaders or fiery prophets...just silence.

What does the world look like when God is quite suddenly and completely silent?

It is important to note just how uncomfortable human nature is with prolonged silence. Yes, we enjoy peace and quiet, but it is rare that we do well with the absence of other voices.

Noisy Children

To illustrate this, let's return to childhood. Remember in elementary school when teachers would turn off the lights and tell us to put our heads down on our desks and be completely quiet? For some reason, quite a few of us found this utterly impossible. If I could keep my face hidden within the circle of my arms I was usually okay, but if I looked about I was in trouble. Someone was always making faces or mouthing words to me, paper footballs were flying, notes were passed, and spitwads were launched to a chorus of muffled whispers and giggles.

I am certain the entire class hated this pause in activity and noise. I know now it existed for the sake of the teacher's sanity. She needed the break, but it was almost impossible to contain ourselves. Why? Because in periods of enforced quiet, the noise within us rises to the surface and begs to gain expression. When the teacher directed our attention and engaged our minds it was easy to stay focused, but when no one was commanding our attention, it was a whole other story. I fear that even though we've grown up, periods of random time-outs are none the easier.

Now imagine the children of Israel for a moment as God's

class. Day after day they are noisy children that the teacher loves—then suddenly He declares a quiet time and actually appears to leave the room. He leaves not for an hour or even a day, but for four hundred years.

Do you remember what happened when the teacher left the room? After posting a lookout, the renegade students took over and the bad behavior began, right? Anything could happen in the teacher's absence! People were hit with erasers. Bra straps were snapped, pencils were stolen, and name-calling began. Mayhem reigned until the lookout gave the warning, "She is coming!"

In an instant all the badly behaved would scamper back to their seats and act as though nothing had happened. There was a flurry of activity as the tracks of mutiny were covered. Of course this was never completely successful. In the midst of the chaos there were some students who were well behaved. This group could be divided into two categories: the good and the goody-two-shoes or tattlers. (I hovered intermittently between bad and good.) These students pleaded with the wild ones to stay in their seats, put the pointer down, keep their hands to themselves, and so on.

More often than not, with the teacher's entrance into the room some clue of calamity was left behind. And the teacher would ask the pointed question, "Who broke my coffee mug?"

The entire group of naughty children would avert their eyes and pray no one would snitch. But there was always one child who could be counted on to tell. Perhaps the teacher would call upon this type, asking, "Lynn, do you know what happened?"

If you were asked it was okay to be truthful or a bit vague. No one expected you to lie, but then there were those who were happy to spill the beans. These were those who would raise their hands and volunteer information, always beginning, of course, by declaring their innocence. "Mrs. So-and-So, I told them to stop but they wouldn't listen. Ricky threw the eraser at Eric and missed and it hit your mug and knocked it off your desk and it broke. And I know you don't know this, but Lisa was out of her chair."

They would always be right but it would all feel so terribly wrong. Snitches gloated with a perverse sense of power as they spilled the secrets of their classmates. They often tattled even before you had a chance to confess. Apparently they lived to get others in trouble!

Tattletales at Work

Now imagine something frightening: four centuries of the tattletales running the religious world! Grasp the horror and you begin to glimpse the oppressive religious atmosphere Mary and Elizabeth lived in.

> *People often take it upon themselves to break the silence and speak on God's behalf.*

When a period of quiet is so long that it becomes uncomfortable and intolerable, people often take it upon themselves to break the silence and speak on God's behalf. More often than not, this is done rather errantly. Without a clear direction from heaven the masses of the self-righteous religious have been known to build elaborate earthly infrastructures, which lay blame and mask the lack of heaven's direct involvement. (I say "direct" because we know God was in fact working on Earth's behalf even in His silence.)

In the days of Mary and Elizabeth, these man-made edifices included exacting and pious regulations in an effort to reach heaven and again earn the favor of God's voice. They knew better than to reconstruct a physical tower of Babel to scale the ominous and oppressive heavenly silence. Instead they created an exclusive "holy only" club. It was a venerable labyrinth, an underground network of complex religious regulations complete with rather ridiculous and elaborate headpieces and titles. Herbs were tithed, greetings in the marketplace were assigned, and boxes of Scriptures were tied to heads. To create support and legal validation, the tattlers surrounded themselves with scribes and lawyers who constructed even more complex lists of rules and ceremonial regulations and before you knew it, the infractions of the masses grew exponentially!

> *There is always a faithful remnant that remembers the spirit behind what God said . . .*

Whenever this happens, history does not paint a flattering picture of mankind. These are often the time periods when we waver between the rigid and religious or the wayward and rebellious. It is when good intentions come up with really bad plans.

The hope and beauty is this: even amid the mess there is always a faithful remnant that remembers the spirit behind what God said even while they uphold the letter. These are those who have not built their own ideas upon the foundation of what God said but choose to lift their eyes from the rubble of yesterday and cling to His promises even if they don't understand His silence.

Survivors of the Silence

Zechariah and Elizabeth were just such people. They lived well and walked uprightly without being mean-spirited.

When Herod was king of Judea, there was a Jewish priest named Zechariah. He was a member of the priestly order of Abijah, and his wife, Elizabeth, was also from the priestly line of Aaron. Zechariah and Elizabeth were righteous in

*God's eyes, careful to obey all of the Lord's commandments
and regulations. They had no children because Elizabeth was
unable to conceive, and they were both very old.* (LUKE 1:5–7)

There are some key points not to be missed in this passage. First, a bad king was in power, but this did not stop God's plan for His earth. No matter what, God will accomplish His purpose.

Second, Zechariah and his wife, Elizabeth, were both descendants of Aaron. In addition to stating the purity of their linage, I believe the mention of both husband and wife foreshadowed how God was restoring the dignity to both genders and setting mothers and fathers in His house. In the days of Moses, the house of Aaron had been promised the honor and covenant of priesthood. To assure this, they were to marry within their tribe to maintain the integrity of this covenant (Leviticus 21:1, 13–14, 22:12–13). The priestly division of Abijah came from the descendents of Aaron's third son, Eleazar, and Aaron's wife was named Elizabeth. Through this strategic couple God was about to restore what had been lost for centuries. If we are making a checklist of qualifications, Elizabeth and Zechariah had the spiritual and natural bloodline.

God was restoring the dignity to both genders and setting mothers and fathers in His house.

The next key point is they were upright in God's sight and blameless before the people. Often when God is silent, people get a little lax in behavior and service, but not Zechariah and Elizabeth. They were well thought of by all.

Even with all this lineage and righteousness going for them, there was one little glitch: no children. They were barren.

BARREN (adjective): Producing no fruit or seed, not able to bear children, infertile, unproductive. A woman who is unable to give birth to children.[1]

The Stigma of Infertility

This account tells us they were not just barren, this couple was "well along in years." Their seasons were nearly fulfilled and they approached the close of life. They had not come of age but were aged and the ability to reproduce was gone. Just how old they were we do not know, but it is certain that like her predecessors Abraham and Sarah, Elizabeth had lost all hope of a child without divine intervention.

According to Jewish thought and custom, if everything was on the up-and-up with your private life and your relationship with God, you should have some babies around. The heritage of children was the proclaimed blessing of the Lord over the couple's life and marriage. If a wife was barren, it was grounds for taking on a second wife!

Regardless of this belief, we see this theme of barren or seemingly infertile women bringing forth life repeated whenever God was ready to begin a new and extraordinary thing. We see closed wombs quickened by God in anticipation of the lives of Isaac, Jacob, Joseph, Samson, and Samuel. It is more than likely that this prolonged period of desolation caused each of these mothers seasons of self-doubt and grief. There was a stigma of reproach tied to a childless, heirless marriage, so we can assume the frustration of barrenness caused all these mothers some level of personal scorn before their children of promise were born.

Those around the aged Elizabeth probably whispered and shook their heads, saying, "Zechariah and Elizabeth seem all right.... Everything seems in order, but they have no children.

Something must be amiss." I know you understand already what I am going to say: people don't like it when their formulas don't work. When something no longer fits into their box of calculations, then they can get a little bit mean and judgmental.

> ## People don't like it when their formulas don't work.

For example, when I first became a Christian, if you were sick it was equated with a lack of faith or the presence of sin in your life. The reasoning of that time said that because God is a healer, if you are not walking in divine health you are out of step with God. I remember the first time I encountered the meanness ("You must be in sin!") behind this proclamation of God's goodness ("God is a healer").

When I was in college, I developed an ear infection. The infection was compounded when I flew to a Christian conference. The pain went from dull to excruciating. When I reached my destination, I asked the other Christians if they could pray for my ear because, to be quite honest, the pain was almost maddening! They gathered around and prayed in earnest. Scriptures were recited, the devil rebuked, and then the responsibility to be healed became mine. I was instructed to thank God for my healing.

I love thanking God, but I was not healed and my ear still hurt. After you'd been prayed for, though, this type of report was strictly forbidden. I also was not allowed to ask for further prayer. I was only allowed to say, "In the natural my ear is in excruciating pain." (Okay, so where else would it hurt—in the spirit?) Or I could say, "I believe I am healed," which also meant I was not yet there, but I was being a good soldier by not negating their prayers with my words. (I know this sounds silly, but bear with me). We all had good intent, we were just a bit confused on how to administer and interpret God's goodness and healing.

I endured two days of indescribable pain, afraid to take Tylenol because it negated my faith with medicine. I confessed every Scripture I knew on healing. Then came the big question: "Lisa, if you believe, why aren't you healed? Could it be there is an area of sin in your life?" Ouch. Just to cover all the bases, I prayed in private and confessed every possible sin I could think of—and still I was no better, I just got worse. Not only was I in pain, I felt like a guilty sinner. I wished I'd stayed in my sorority rather than attending the conference. At least there I would have experienced the benefit of rest and pain medication without accusation.

It was wonderful to feel free of the incessant judgment of others.

On Saturday night of the conference, everything changed. At the close of the service the speaker prayed a mass prayer for healing. The minister instructed us to lay our hands on whatever areas were bothering us. I casually slipped my hand up to my ear, he prayed, and my ear literally popped open and every trace of pain disappeared. I could hear perfectly and began to cry with relief. It was great to be healed, great to experience God's goodness, but even more than all these it was wonderful to feel free of the incessant judgment of others.

Mine was just a three-day struggle, but Elizabeth suffered for years! Don't you think infertile women go through enough pain and self-doubt without the sisters in the church whispering and hypothesizing why they're barren? None of us are good enough to earn the beauty of God's blessing and provision. I did everything wrong and was blessed with four beautiful children. Yet I know women who did everything right and they struggled with infertility or suffered miscarriages. We need to get God's perspective.

> *The barren woman has a houseful of children, while the mother of many is bereft.* (1 SAMUEL 2:5 THE MESSAGE)

God will use a barren season of life to increase our capacity for more. Hannah cried out for a single child and in addition to Samuel the prophet, she was given a household. Likewise everything was getting ready to change for the elderly, upright Zechariah and Elizabeth. The time was coming when all the whispering would change to gasps of wonder.

An Angel Speaks

> *One day Zechariah was serving God in the Temple, for his order was on duty that week. As was the custom of the priests, he was chosen by lot to enter the sanctuary of the Lord and burn incense. While the incense was being burned, a great crowd stood outside, praying.* (LUKE 1:8–10)

Notice the "on duty that week"; Zechariah had been on duty before, but this time it was his turn to go into God's holy place. Zechariah was singled out from among his division by lot and called to go alone into the holy place while outside, in the courts of God, the worshipers lifted up prayers. The priest offered the holy incense, which symbolized the ascension and fragrance of prayer.

The crowd watched as he entered the holy place. While he prepared to do the ritual, something extraordinary happened.

Don't Be Afraid

While Zechariah was in the sanctuary, an angel of the Lord appeared to him, standing to the right of the incense altar. Zechariah was shaken and overwhelmed with fear when he saw him. (LUKE 1:11–12)

Zechariah walked into the temple and found he was not alone. I always find the human reaction to angels amazing and a bit humorous. This angel appeared and waited for Zechariah's reaction—and react he did with shock and awe at the sight of this marvelous heavenly being. After four hundred years of nothing, suddenly there was an angel at the altar.

But the angel said, "Don't be afraid, Zechariah!" (LUKE 1:13)

What does this "But" mean here? I think it means the large angel who was before Zechariah understood that the small human was completely terrified, "but" they needed to talk, so he should relax. The phrase "Don't be afraid" seems to be consistently part of the introduction when angels encounter humans. They know they terrify people, so to add some warmth and calm us down, they call us by name.

Fear must always first be confronted before any promise of heaven can be heard on Earth.

Or is it that an even more important truth is hidden in this greeting? I believe there is something really big hidden in the words "Do not be afraid." You see, fear must always first be confronted before any promise of heaven can be heard on Earth. If you are captive to fear, you cannot truly hear or bear what God is about to say. Instead of listening and allowing God's message to enlarge your life, you are too overwhelmed by trying to figure out how it will happen and what it will look like, and compiling a list of reasons why you can't do it. In that frame of mind, it is impossible to just open up and experience the wonder of it all.

The angel continued to address Zechariah.

You Have Been Heard

God has heard your prayer. (LUKE 1:13)

If an angel said this to me, I would have a meltdown. I would hit my knees and weep. Imagine, after four hundred years of a brass heaven, my prayer was the first one to be heard! I hope I would just be saying, "Thank You, God, thank You, God!"

I mean, think of it! The angel was present or (pre-sent) to confirm God's response to Zechariah's personal prayer. What this aged priest had whispered and cried for in secret had reached the throne and courts of heaven. The fact heaven responded was such a big deal an angel was delivering the answer to his petition.

Surprisingly, the angel made no mention of the corporate prayers, which at that moment were ascending before God's throne. He didn't say, "The prayers of God's assembled people have been heard"! No, God made it personal with Zechariah.

Whenever God begins to do something big on Earth, He uses individuals who are willing to let Him get intimately involved in their lives.

There is another point here that should encourage each and every one of us: whenever God begins to do something big on Earth, He uses individuals who are willing to let Him get intimately involved in their lives. I believe He was foreshadowing the rending of the veil and His promise to engage with each of us one on one.

So what was the old priest's prayer that got God's attention? He wanted a son; he wanted laughter and a legacy to live beyond his earthly life. This longing and prayer were heard and the angel expounded on how the answer would be fulfilled.

You Will Have a Son

Your wife, Elizabeth, will give you a son, and you are to name him John. You will have great joy and gladness, and many will rejoice at his birth, for he will be great in the eyes of the Lord. (Luke 1:13–15)

God was going to fill Zechariah's life with joy and delight—that portion of the angel's announcement was the personal fulfillment. Then this son of delight would one day extend his reach far beyond their family of three as he declared truth in the lives of others. Many would rejoice at his birth because this son would be "great in the eyes of the Lord." A lot of people are great in the sight of each other, but what an honor to be declared great by God. Within the answer to Zechariah's prayer was the fulfillment of a four-hundred-year-old promise and prophecy that would be the answer to the prayers of many.

Do you hear this? You see, you may never know what is actually in your personal prayer until it is answered. A prayer for a son or a daughter may be about a whole lot more than your having a child. Your prayer for a lost loved one may be a whole lot bigger than that person's not going to hell. Your business' success may have a whole lot more to do than you know with heaven's purpose.

God loves it when we pray gut-level, authentic prayers. It gives Him some earthen "dirt" to work with. God has always taken the dirt and made something beautiful out of it. When we draw near and are honest, God can turn around our issues and then take what blesses and heals us on an individual basis and magnify it for the healing of many—sometimes even for the healing of nations. I doubt you could even contain the wonder of all God wants to do with and through your prayers.

God loves it when we pray gut-level, authentic prayers.

I have seen this proven true in my own life. For years I cried out for freedom from fear, guilt, and shame. I did not ask God to set me free so He could free others through me. It was completely about me. "God, set me free! Here is all my dirt and shame—have Your way." But His answer to this captive daughter's plea in time expanded and brought healing and release to the lives of other similarly captive daughters around the world.

My husband, John, prayed for years for God to give him a ministry and a voice to the nations and, to be quite honest, very little happened. Then he was emotionally and spiritually wounded, and as he struggled to overcome this injury, the focus of his life and prayers began to change. It was not until he cried out for healing from an offense that he found his restoration and voice of ministry released.

I am not suggesting for a moment that we stop praying for others. We need to do this in ever-increasing measures. I am just suggesting there are times when massive, world-changing forces of life are born from our personal anguish. The cry of one who is hurting gives birth to something so much bigger than we can imagine or contain. God loves it when you are honest with Him. I don't know the pain and barrenness in your life...but could they be like Hannah's cry? The quickening of life within you may be the answer to prayers of a nation.

> *There are times when massive, world-changing forces of life are born from our personal anguish.*

Because this heaven-sent child would do extraordinary things, the angel gave specific instructions to Zechariah on how this forerunner was to be raised.

He Will Be Filled with the Holy Spirit

He must never touch wine or other alcoholic drinks. He will be filled with the Holy Spirit, even before his birth. And he will turn many Israelites to the Lord their God. He will be a man with the spirit and power of Elijah. He will prepare the people for the coming of the Lord. He will turn the hearts of the fathers to their children, and he will cause those who are rebellious to accept the wisdom of the godly. (LUKE 1:15–17)

He would be filled with the Spirit even before he drew his first breath. He was never to have fermented drink. Why? The Spirit would be his wine. He was the anointed one to turn the hearts of the fathers to their children and the disobedient to wisdom, thus preparing a people to receive the revelation of the Lord. It sounds like a done deal, but for some reason I am not sure Zechariah was completely capable of hearing it all. Apparently he was still a bit tripped up with angel shock and the age issue, because after everything he had heard it was the only thing he thought to question.

Let's be honest: he could have raised a whole course of questions! There must have been a pause because he said something rather stupid.

You Will Be Silent

Zechariah said to the angel, "How can I be sure this will happen? I'm an old man now, and my wife is also well along in years."

(LUKE 1:18)

Okay, this is not good. I am not sure he was thinking when he asked this one. It makes me wonder if in the presence of angels, whatever you're wrestling in your mind, no matter how random, just comes out of your mouth before you can stop it. (Remember how Peter said something stupid as well about setting up tents when the glory fell on the Mount of Transfiguration?) Perhaps this glorious news was too much wonder for Zechariah to take in.

In my opinion, Zechariah had the easy part. It was Elizabeth who should have asked some questions! As I sit and read this account from the relatively safe position of observer, it all seems rather obvious: every time an angel appears, it's a sure thing. Sarah laughed and still got pregnant, but perhaps Zechariah was having some difficulty processing the Abraham dynamic in his life and called himself "old" and his wife "well along in years." I think it is cute that even back then men knew better than to describe their wives as "old." Regardless of what I think, the angel did not think it was cute that Zechariah asked for a sign to assure his words.

Then the angel said, "I am Gabriel! I stand in the very presence of God. It was he who sent me to bring you this good news!"

(LUKE 1:19)

In most biblical angelic encounters, angels didn't give out their names. This one not only volunteered his name, but he described his proximity to God as well. The angel Gabriel was not an outer-court angel that occasionally came into God's presence for a visit. He stood (stands) in the very presence of the Most High. His name did not mean "messenger," as most assume; *Gabriel* means "mighty of God."[2] Just by uttering his name he declared God's omnipotence. The angel Gabriel left God's holy presence only when sent directly by the Lord Most High.

> *But now, since you didn't believe what I said, you will be silent and unable to speak until the child is born. For my words will certainly be fulfilled at the proper time.* (LUKE 1:20)

Questioning the angel was the last opportunity Zechariah had to speak for quite a while, because Gabriel shut his mouth.

If you resist God, you risk losing your voice.

In this interchange we find another spiritual principle revealed. If you resist God, you risk losing your voice.

When God Removes Your Voice

Over the years I have witnessed this dynamic in one form or another. There was a very influential pastor who was oppressive of women—women were not allowed to lead or to speak in any capacity to men. John and I were out with some other pastors who had observed this when he spoke at a conference they had hosted. They were all alarmed and brought their concern to our attention. In the midst of the conversation someone said, "If he does not stop oppressing women, God will shut his mouth."

A hush settled over all of us. Later that night John and I discussed it in our hotel room. Both of us had sensed a shift in the Spirit. It was as though a line had been drawn. Within a few weeks the pastor's voice was silenced.

Zechariah learned a lesson we would all do well to heed: agree with what God is doing. Believe what He is saying. Let the Spirit, not the letter of the Word, always be the final authority in your life. And in the process, remain humble and teachable.

In over twenty years of ministry experience and close observation, I've seen this played out repeatedly. If you oppose what God is doing or saying, you run the risk of spiritual laryngitis. If you are wise and make adjustments as needed, the silence will last only for a season.

Sometimes this means you will no longer have a voice that is heard on a larger scale. Other times it will mean your words will become irrelevant, indistinct, and uncertain because the conditions of your personal private life will interfere with what you declare publicly. Or in the case of the minister who dishonored women, you may lose credibility and platform until you repent. We must all be careful lest we resist what God is doing and merely defend what He has done. God is always doing a new thing that brings new life. In the time of Zechariah, God was birthing a new voice from an old vessel.

God's Answer, God's Timing

The angel gave Zechariah the assurance and the sign he requested. He would remain silent until the fulfillment of the angel's word and the promise was brought forth. It is important to note that God answers our prayers in His timing.

We forget to factor in heaven's perspective.

Because of the way Zechariah answered the angel, I am quite certain he had given up all hope of a son. In fact, even though he went home silent he may have returned to his wife equally overjoyed a son was on his way! Often we mistakenly think when our prayers are not answered in our timing or even in our lifetime that they have gone unanswered. We assume this because we forget to factor in heaven's perspective. Frequently we have the privilege of sending our prayers ahead of us and then the answers come in our children's lifetimes rather than ours.

> *Meanwhile, the people were waiting for Zechariah to come out of the sanctuary, wondering why he was taking so long. When he finally did come out, he couldn't speak to them. Then they realized from his gestures and his silence that he must have seen a vision in the sanctuary.* (LUKE 1:21–22)

When someone comes out of God's presence speechless, people take notice. If things had been different, Zechariah might have been able to come out and declare that heaven was open, that their prayers were being answered, that God was aligning Earth and heaven, and that the promises of the ages was upon them. Of course none of this happened. He made signs with his hands but was unable to speak or explain what had transpired. Isn't it wonderful that even when we blow things, God gives us the privilege of still pointing others in the right direction?

Elizabeth's Response

> *When Zechariah's week of service in the Temple was over, he returned home. Soon afterward his wife, Elizabeth, became pregnant and went into seclusion for five months. "How kind the Lord is!" she exclaimed. "He has taken away my disgrace of having no children."* (LUKE 1:23–25)

Zechariah went home to his wife, they had sex, and she became pregnant. But instead of making a public announcement, she did something very interesting: she went into hiding!

For the first five months she stayed in "seclusion." If I were Elizabeth and I finally became pregnant after decades of waiting, I don't know if I would have been godly enough to go into seclusion. Do you hear her words? "How kind the Lord is! He has taken away my disgrace of having no children." After years of disgrace I would have been ready to be vindicated! I probably would have been hanging out at the well and shopping conspicuously at the marketplace to make sure everyone was keeping track of my expanding belly! If people didn't notice, I probably would have pointed it all out: "Hey, in case you didn't notice I'm pregnant and my husband isn't talking anymore. I think God is doing something with us! It sounds as though this baby may be the Elijah to come. Aren't you sorry you whispered about us these past twenty plus years?"

Do you see how amazing this woman was? She didn't flaunt God's goodness toward her. She drew near to Him in sanctification. You see, Elizabeth got something most people miss. She understood that the amazing life growing within her would soon pass through her. The pregnancy was not about her. She knew it was about so much more. When Elizabeth became pregnant, I believe she was quickened with the revelation and realization that God was fulfilling her name. Why do I say this? The name *Elizabeth* means "consecrated to God."[3]

Elizabeth did more than just eat ice cream
and hummus. She chose an increased
level of personal sanctification.

The angel Gabriel had said John was to be set apart and sanctified, but Elizabeth did more than just eat ice cream and hummus. She chose an increased level of personal sanctification and took the promise of God into hiding. She was a once-barren woman about to give to birth to the prophetic and while she contemplated what exactly that might mean in the life of an aged woman, God sent Gabriel forth again.

The Angel and Mary

In the sixth month of Elizabeth's pregnancy, God sent the angel Gabriel to Nazareth, a village in Galilee, to a virgin named Mary. She was engaged to be married to a man named Joseph, a descendant of King David. (LUKE 1:26–27)

"In the sixth month" refers to the gestation timetable of Elizabeth's pregnancy. She was well along with child and obviously showing when the angel Gabriel was sent to Nazareth. Through the womb of Elizabeth, the appearance of Jesus' prophetic forerunner was already set in motion. God had set the stage for the miraculous by accomplishing the humanly impossible.

Now God was preparing the way for the promised root of David who would be King. Gabriel appeared to a young virgin of the lineage of David whose name was Mary or Miriam. The meaning of her name is a bit muddy. It would seem originally the name *Mary* or *Miriam* meant "beloved," but during the Israelites' sojourn in the wilderness it took on the meaning of "rebellious" to its original "beloved" or "favored"? [4] Perhaps this encounter is very poignant on a personal level for Mary. . . . Is the meaning of her name being reversed from "rebellious" to "favored" or is God speaking prophetically to all, announcing that those who were once considered rebels (the Gentiles) would earn favor through the sacrifice of Emmanuel?

Since when has God been with those called "rebellious"? Food for thought!

The Lord Is with You

> *Gabriel appeared to her and said, "Greetings, favored woman! The Lord is with you!" Confused and disturbed, Mary tried to think what the angel could mean.* (LUKE 1:28–29)

Zechariah was "shaken and overwhelmed with fear" by Gabriel's presence and Mary was "confused and disturbed" at his words. The angel did more than call her by name, he seemed to reverse the meaning of her name, saying, "Highly favored one, God is with you!"

Okay, pause a moment and remember our time period. The faultfinding tattletales were in charge, and when religion was mean, it was really mean to women. In that culture, women were not valued. In light of this there are some confusing and troubling things here.

First, women were rarely considered highly favored. If, in fact, they were fortunate enough to find favor with people, it was almost unheard of for them to be favored by God. Then Gabriel showed up and declared "God is with you" to a poor young girl betrothed to a man of little or no influence!

Do you know why this is so important? I believe God is declaring His presence and favor over a generation of daughters who are divinely destined to carry the gospel of Emmanuel throughout the world.

He is preparing to allow us to personally partner with Him in what He is doing on the earth.

Pause and consider this, you whose hearts are quickened. Beautiful daughter, I hear these words declared over your life even now. God is with His highly favored daughters born for such a time and purpose as this. What does it mean when God begins to call forth His people by name? He is preparing to allow us to personally partner with Him in what He is doing on the earth.

You Have Found Favor with God

"Don't be afraid, Mary," the angel told her, "for you have found favor with God! You will conceive and give birth to a son, and you will name him Jesus. He will be very great and will be called the Son of the Most High. The Lord God will give him the throne of his ancestor David. And he will reign over Israel forever; his Kingdom will never end!"

(LUKE 1:29–33)

Just like Zechariah, Mary was told, "Don't be afraid." The admonishment could be paraphrased as "Don't be frightened. God highly favors you!" This virgin was going to be with child and give birth to God's Son, and through Him David's throne would again be established. She received the angel's words with joy but there remained the nagging question of how.

Mary asked the angel, "But how can this happen? I am a virgin." (LUKE 1:34)

Mary's question did not test the angel's patience and she received an answer without rebuke.

The angel replied, "The Holy Spirit will come upon you, and the power of the Most High will overshadow you. So the baby to be born will be holy, and he will be called the Son of God." (LUKE 1:35)

This time life would not spring forth from a barren place, it would kindle in a virgin womb. A virgin womb is completely enclosed and represents that which is pure and untainted. For an example, virgin olive oil comes from the first pressing of the seed without the introduction of heat. The power of God would overshadow Mary and life would begin.

Then the angel gave the validation for his declaration:

> *What's more, your relative Elizabeth has become pregnant in her old age! People used to say she was barren, but she's now in her sixth month. For nothing is impossible with God.*
>
> (LUKE 1:36–37)

The example of Elizabeth was given to encourage Mary. Obviously Elizabeth kept her pregnancy so private that even her relatives did not know about the promise growing inside her. God had set up the miraculous with the impossible.

God had set up the miraculous with the impossible.

Mary's Response

> *Mary responded, "I am the Lord's servant. May everything you have said about me come true." And then the angel left her.*
>
> (LUKE 1:38)

This is the position and response of highly favored daughters. I am going to take the liberty of paraphrasing it here so you can make this simple and profound response of Mary's your own: *I am God's highly favored daughter. May everything He says about me come true.*

What did Mary do with this amazing news? She ran to Eliza-

beth. The highly favored daughter sought the company of a consecrated grandmother and a beautiful interchange occurred.

*A few days later Mary hurried to the hill country of Judea,
to the town where Zechariah lived. She entered the house
and greeted Elizabeth. At the sound of Mary's greeting, Elizabeth's child leaped within her, and Elizabeth was filled with
the Holy Spirit.*   (LUKE 1:39–41)

At the sound of Mary's voice, the life within Elizabeth leapt
and "Elizabeth was filled with the Holy Spirit." The promise
was that the baby within would be filled, but this blessing
spilled over to his mother who had positioned herself to receive. Elizabeth did what women who are filled with the Holy
Spirit are meant to do: she blessed.

*Elizabeth gave a glad cry and exclaimed to Mary, "God
has blessed you above all women, and your child is blessed.
Why am I so honored, that the mother of my Lord should
visit me? When I heard your greeting, the baby in my womb
jumped for joy. You are blessed because you believed that the
Lord would do what he said."*   (LUKE 1:42–45)

In her words we find the blessing mothers and grandmothers should release over the daughters of God: Blessed is *she*
who believes that what the Lord has said *to her* will be accomplished. Daughter, what has God said to you? Make it personal
and believe it.

Daughter, what has God said to you?

After this interchange, Mary stayed with Elizabeth until
her time of delivery. The prophetic and the promise pondered

life together. We don't know what instruction and fellowship transpired between these two women so filled with life, but I want you to ponder some of the following truths about mothers, grandmothers, and daughters.

- God-related women, regardless of age, are going to conceive and bring forth life.
- The consecrated and the highly favored are going to echo God's Word to each other.
- The mothers and grandmothers must listen for the sound of the daughters' voices and bless them when they hear them.
- The daughters should honor the mothers and grandmothers by lending their youthful strength as they are trained and instructed.
- The prophetic and the promise will run together in the last days.

God is positioning His daughters of all ages through declarative words and revelatory insights. Together we will create a type of synergy, but to see this happen well we must be trained. In the next chapter we will review what that interchange looks like.

9

Training

TRAIN (verb): To learn or teach the necessary skills, especially through practical experience. To make a plant, bush or tree grow in a particular way by pruning or tying. To aim something.[1]

We women are in a season of great upheaval and transition on every level. The climate of everything from the family to our world is changing. There is a vast disparity between the way things are and the way things should be. If we will stretch and choose to be a part of this restoration we will be amazed at the richness and joy it brings into our lives. (Just an aside for my older sisters: I promise this change of focus renews your youth!)

Similarly, teach the older women to live in a way that honors God. They must not slander others or be heavy drinkers. Instead, they should teach others what is good. These older women must train the younger women to love their husbands and their children, to live wisely and be pure, to work in their homes, to do good, and to be submissive to their husbands. Then they will not bring shame on the word of God.

(TITUS 2:3–5)

Reviewing the words of Titus, we can conclude life must not have been altogether different for the first-century church. It appears the daughters were being trained as the mothers were being taught.

None of us have arrived yet. There is still so much to learn and unlearn that we must allow room for growth and forgiveness. There is still so much disparity between the way things are and the way they should be that if we are to find our way, both the young and the not-so-young must start on this path and meet one another on a higher plane of truth.

An Older Woman's Role

Live in a Way That Honors God

Older women are first admonished to be an example of what is appropriate for those who serve God. If you are wondering if you qualify as "older"...just figure you are always older than someone. This charge means our lives should not be a contradiction to truth.

> ### Whether you "signed up" to be an example or not, you are one.

We can draw an inescapable conclusion: the older women are being watched by the younger. Whether you "signed up" to be an example or not, you are one.

Not long ago I attended a pastors' wives conference. To be quite frank, there was an incredible amount of whining about how they all hated being on display. They expressed resentment about being watched and critiqued by their congregation women. There was a chorus of loud "amens" as fellow pastor wives affirmed this common problem. I grew increasingly uncomfortable, but I wasn't sure why.

It wasn't until another pastor's wife spoke and volunteered a very different perspective then I understood my discomfort. Yes, she affirmed, they were all being watched, but that was not necessarily a bad thing. You see, more often than not, the daughters in the house of God are not watching for the mothers in that house to fail; on the contrary, they are desperately watching for them to succeed!

Your victories are light and hope to another.

When I watch Joyce Meyer's program, *Enjoying Everyday Life*, I don't turn it on to see where she is going to mess up. I tune in to glean how she has learned to live so well after so much personal hardship. Joyce's successes are the promise of potential to every other daughter of God. The same is true of you. Your victories are light and hope to another.

You have incredible potential to influence for good and godliness because you are being watched. I know the young girls on our staff watch everything I do. This ranges from the way I speak to my husband to how I dress and style my hair. It is a given that they are watching...what are we modeling? It's time the older women took back the role of supermodel!

On the flip side, when we've set a bad example and have not worn a situation well, we need to own it. I can't even count the number of times I have had to turn to my assistant and apologize. Then I get the joyous task of explaining how I could have handled the situation better. My life is an example to her. Every day the choice is mine: will I be a good example or an object lesson? Believe me, it is better to lead by example than by embarrassment! Either way I cannot escape her watchful eyes.

> **Believe me, it is better to lead by**
> **example than by embarrassment!**

Let's continue to break down the Titus directive.

Don't Slander Others

As mothers in the house of God, we are not to slander or speak evil of others. I know this is hard because there is such a vast store of information in the life of the mature. Some details of the things we've seen would best remain unsaid. There are still ways to glean the good from the bad. The truth is, between the Bible and my personal failures I have more than enough material from which to instruct others. I don't need to critique other sisters or play the drama queen and paint myself a victim.

Women are God's hand-picked connecters. If we are not schooled in "good" and likewise healthy and empowered, we will frequently use our words inappropriately. Older women have the weight of years added to their words, so we must be more judicious with our distribution of information. The catty behavior that is acceptable and normal in middle and high school is not even a consideration for mothers in the house of God.

Don't Drink Heavily

Next, older women are not to be heavy drinkers. Okay, it has been a while since I was drunk, but I distinctly remember it caused me to say and do stupid things. Remember how people get information in the movies? They get the informant drunk and he unwittingly spills secrets as he loses all discretion. I personally say enough stupid things without the introduction of heavy drinking or drunkenness.

Teach Goodness

Paul went on to say we are to teach that which is good. I like the simplicity of this. God wants us to focus on "good," not the doctrinally complex or fancy. We don't need to give voice to the bad...just the good. Here was Paul's list of good things to teach:

1. Love your husband and children.
2. Live wisely.
3. Be pure.
4. Take care of your home.
5. Be submissive.

We will cover the issue of the home at length in another chapter, so we will not address it here. We will cover the other areas, though. I am afraid that for far too long women have exemplified but a fraction of the "good" God intended. From this charge in Titus and various verses in Proverbs, we could infer that women are the guardians of good. Why do I think this? Because you would never logically charge someone to teach what has not been entrusted to his or her care. (Paul was rather big on logic.) Loving your husband is good. Loving your children is good. Loving your friends is good. Serving is good. Generosity is good. Wisdom is good. Purity is another thing that is good. Taking care of your home and making it a place of beauty, rest, and hospitality for your family is good. Being kind, inclusive, and polite is good.

As mothers we need to ask ourselves how often daughters learn the hard way lessons we could have made easier if we'd opened our hearts and lives and instructed them. The truth is, none of us were meant to struggle or to figure it all out alone.

Train the Younger

Look again at Titus 2:4:

These older women must train the younger women…

Older women *must* train the younger. "Must" is a strong word that does not leave room for opting out. Older women, how can we despise the ignorance of the younger if we have neglected their training? Ultimately they are a reflection of us. Paul's words were not a suggestion, but a mandate. I often wonder if the reason we have not trained is because far too often our training was neglected as well. Or, if we did enjoy the benefit of godly counsel and wisdom, we chose the counsel of our peers over the counsel of older, wiser women. How many older women are intimidated by the beauty of the young and have forgotten how quickly the flower of youth fades if it is not cultivated and grown into something more?

> **Even though I never had spiritual mothering or even mentoring, God still requires I be that woman to the daughters.**

In my youth, I watched and waited, hoping a godly woman would deem me worthy of her time and instruction, but it just did not happen. Now I am actually thankful for this dynamic, because I believe God wanted to weave a deeper level of brokenness and dependence into the fabric of my life. Even though I never had spiritual mothering or even mentoring, God still requires I be woman to the daughters.

He does not say, "Mother, you must train your daughter." He laid this charge on *all* older females. We are required to reach out to the young women and if He requires this of us, then He will empower us for the task before us.

More often than not, He is asking a generation of mother-less daughters to be mothers! Nothing changes until one generation of women rises up beyond what they have known and seen and makes the declaration, no matter the cost, "There must be change! I will stand in the gap. It no longer matters what I had or did not have in my life. I want something more for the daughters who now surround me. I want something more for my friends who live in perpetual pain. I want to love well and teach others to love and be well loved."

> *When we invite others in, not only do we find our*
> *worlds enlarged, we find our capacities increased.*

It doesn't change until girls in their late teens or early twenties begin to speak words of truth and life to the preteen sisters who admire them. It does not change until those who've been grasping for help reach out to raise others. When we invite others in, not only do we find our worlds enlarged, we find our capacities increased.

Train the Younger To. . . .

Let's review the points continued in Paul's charge.

Love Your Husband

LOVE (verb): To feel tender affection for somebody, for example, a close relative or friend. To feel romantic and sexual desire and longing for somebody. To feel and show kindness and charity to somebody.[2]

You may wonder why Paul exhorted us to love our husbands. Isn't that something wives do naturally? The current rate of divorce would say otherwise. I am not sure whether it is a breakdown in intentional instruction or if there is a lack of modeling love in our homes, but something is desperately wrong. Earlier this week, a sincere young girl asked me, "Why should I even hope to have a successful, joy-filled marriage? When I look around, all I see is Christians who are just sticking their marriage out or divorcing. Where is the hope in that?"

Paul did not say, "Just stay married"...he said, "Love your husbands." There can be love. I have been married for more than twenty-five years and I love my husband more today than I did when we were even dating. But what exactly is love? Is it the fluttery feeling? Sometimes...but it even runs deeper. Sometimes there is no evident feeling, only a consistent choice: *I will love—not tolerate, endure, or merely live with, but love.*

For years I have grieved over the divorce rate in the church. I've watched uncomfortably as older men have tossed aside the wives of their youth for youthful wives (ones in the age range of their children). I've seen the hurt and confusion in the eyes of ex-wives and children. I've witnessed an almost arrogant demeanor as ex-husbands flaunted their new, improved versions before the local church body.

I've even threatened to shoot John to keep him from committing such a grievous error. But in all sincerity, it's frightening. I've had to resist the urge to ask the young woman, "What are you thinking? You have destroyed another woman's life and home!"

I was so troubled I sought God and in His presence I gained a sense that the current church divorce crisis is at least linked to the breakdown between the older and younger women.

If older women are commanded to teach the young women and they neglect this charge, what do they inherit? Perhaps it is frightened, foolish, willful daughters. Could these be the very ones who lack discretion and decide if they can't have the nurture of a mother, they will marry the security of a father? If they have not been trained to love, they will do what is necessary to survive.

They want to be taken care of. If growing up and growing old together with a husband with whom you have children is not an exciting and joyful option, then they might as well specialize in taking care of themselves. Please understand, there is a flip side to this as well. I know wives abandon their husbands and children, but this is far less prevalent.

If they have not been trained to love, they will do what is necessary to survive.

When a link is weak, the whole chain suffers. I am raising questions here, not claiming to have complete answers. I am in no way implying that women who suffer the abandonment and betrayal of divorce are at fault because they *personally* did not do something. No, the truth is neglect has permeated the mind-set and demographics of our culture. When something is this far amiss, it affects everyone. I know there are godly women who poured into the lives of young women and still found themselves abandoned and alone.

Because we want to be agents of change, let's break down some practical lessons from Titus. I'm going to open a window on some things in the next few sections I have learned by trial and error so you can have some real-life examples.

How to love your husband. Men are most fulfilled when you love them the way they want to be loved. For years I did not get this. I wanted to love John the way I liked to be loved. Men often communicate love differently than women, and an excellent book to help you interpret these various dialects is one called

The Five Love Languages: How to Express Heartfelt Commitment to Your Mate by Gary Chapman (Northfield, 1995).

Here is an example of my love communication breakdown. My major ways of showing love: quality time and acts of service. (I am personally convinced these are the love languages of Jesus.) This meant I was busy doing things (laundry, cooking, cleaning, painting, gardening) for my husband and kids to show my abundant love for them. I also spent large portions of time with them doing things I felt spelled *love*. I attempted deep, meaningful conversations as I organized closets, painted walls, and so on.

My husband was not on the same page with me. He was not hearing what I was saying. First, he was rarely home long enough to spend quality time and when he was home, he was more interested in resting than collaborating on a project. So as I pulled up carpet and laid tile, thinking these acts loudly and clearly declared "I love you," he heard nothing. I cooked a big meal and he didn't hear love expressed. Why?

None of these made him feel loved. He was looking for some words of affirmation...which I thought was absolutely ridiculous! I mean, the man traveled all over the place being affirmed by clapping crowds. I needed to keep him humble. Right?

Wrong! He didn't care what anyone else said about him; he wanted to know that I would say. I was the voice that mattered most. I began to change my approach. At first it felt awkward, then it just became fun. In front of our boys I began to say, "John Bevere, you're a sexy hunk of man!" John would smile shyly. My boys would protest, saying "TMI!" but I would not be deterred. You see, a couple of things were happening in this interchange. John was being built up and my boys were learning how they should be treated by their wives.

For a marriage to be healthy, both people should be happy

and well loved. In light of this, there is nothing wrong with letting each other know how you hear love communicated. So you have the right to be heard as well because when you feel loved, you are better equipped to love well. This conversation is best done in a kind, nonaccusing way. It might sound something like, "I feel loved when you . . ." and then elaborate.

> ### *When you feel loved, you are*
> ### *better equipped to love well.*

When you have this conversation, you can expect little or no results if you are running down a list of faults and then tack on your preferences. Take it from me, it just doesn't work. Your husband will check out while you are still talking. His thoughts will be something like this: *I can't please her no matter what I do. I am going to quit trying!* This is exactly the opposite of what you want to have happen, so don't adopt this approach.

Another important aspect of loving your husband has to do with when you try to communicate with him. One mistake I made was attempting huge discussions at bedtime when we were both exhausted. Timing is everything. Something that could be discussed civilly in the morning may start a fight when you are both tired.

Late at night is also not a good time to plan out the next day. I am not even capable of making good decisions when I am utterly exhausted. Early in my marriage, I wanted the next day's details off my mind, so I would try to make plans, and if John was tired he would just go along with the suggestion. "John, will you pick up the boys tomorrow? I have a major appointment."

"Sure."

The only problem was the next day he did not even remember what he agreed to. I, of course, took this as rejection. Why didn't he think what I thought was important was important? Obviously he was not considerate of me!

Well, the truth is John forgets almost everything I tell him at night. Life goes so much smoother when we discuss things midmorning with pen and paper in hand. If it is important, then say it at the best time for it to be heard. I understand there are emergencies and sometimes this is just not feasible, but I used to dump on my husband every night. I probably unloaded on him so I could sleep, but after a few years of night-fights, I learned this doesn't work.

Love Your Children

Again, I'll share some things I learned the hard way.

Training. One of the best ways you can love your children is to be consistent. I began motherhood madly in love with my babies and soon found myself overwhelmed and just mad! I never stopped loving my children, but I was angry at myself for not doing a better job at mothering. I was frustrated because I could not manage to teach my children to listen the first time. I couldn't believe how long this made the simplest of tasks. Often the burden to do everything fell on me!

Then one night it all changed—because I changed. I repented and began to honor God's Word in my approach to raising my children. For example, I told them something one time, and if I was not obeyed there was consequence.

When my sons were older and no longer appreciated my doing their laundry, I trained them to do their own. You may be wondering what boy wouldn't appreciate his mother doing the laundry. Answer: thirteen- and eleven-year-olds. I had found folded clean clothes thrown into the dirty laundry hamper one too many times. I warned them if they did not put away their clothes properly and continued to make more work for me, I would stop doing the wash for them.

I remember the day I walked them downstairs and introduced them to the washer and dryer. I taught them how to separate their clothes, set the washer and dryer, and how to use detergent and fabric softener. Then I left it to them.

Yes, I endured complaints such as, all the other mothers do their children's laundry! Don't be swayed: there is nothing wrong with your children doing their own laundry and carrying some of the weight around the house. Why should moms be stressed out and neglect the training of their children in the process? You are not called to be their maid; you are called to be their mother and to train them in how to live with others and walk in godliness.

> **You are not called to be their maid;**
> **you are called to be their mother.**

Young mother, I know you do a better job picking up the toys than they do, but how will they ever learn if you always do it for them? Teach them to do it until they get it right. At first this is exhausting. You'll be tempted to think, *It is just not worth it! I'll just do it for them!* If you give in, though, guess who is training whom? Your children are smart enough to know how to wear you down.

Calmly explain what you expect to be done and how much time you are going to allot for them to do it. Then set the timer. Make the buzzer the bad guy. Inspect progress regularly and give additional instruction when necessary until it is done. If they refuse to follow through in a timely manner, then discipline is required.

Those who spare the rod of discipline hate their children. Those who love their children care enough to discipline them. (PROVERBS 13:24)

170

Why are we careful to discipline our children? It is all part of their training and a very real part of being a parent. Even God disciplines the children He loves. Why? So we can be partakers of His divine nature. Without discipline you will not get the things of God. Undisciplined children ultimately shame their parents.

> To discipline a child produces wisdom, but a mother is disgraced by an undisciplined child.   (PROVERBS 29:15)

> A youngster's heart is filled with foolishness, but physical discipline will drive it far away.   (PROVERBS 22:15)

So many children grow up without a work ethic because they never learn one at home. I cook each night and my boys all help with the clean-up. Even when they were young, they had little jobs. If you get them started early enough, they will do chores out of habit: clear the plates, sweep the floors, wipe the table. Young children can do all these.

Problems arise when you don't start them out helping and then try to make it happen once they're trained to be served rather than to be servants. We should raise our children to be people who know how to work alongside others.

If you have started out wrong, have a heart-to-heart with your kids and make the adjustments today. I literally sat my sons down one day and said, "Hey, God showed me I have been doing it all wrong. But from this point forward, we are going to do it right. Mommy is going to let you guys be helpers. I will not yell anymore. I will say it one time and you will do it—understood?"

Engaging. If you have more than one child, you are already aware how different each child is. For the most part, my boys are aggressively—and I do mean *aggressively* in a literal sense—engaged with us. They enjoy wrestling, picking me up and carrying me off, etc. But as the seasons of their lives grow and expand, I have seen them wander. I would sense a pulling away here or there.

At first I was confused: *Why is this child withdrawing from us?* Because of all the noise and activity in my house, I sometimes did not even notice it until later. I would be in bed thinking, *Did I kiss him good night? ... When did he slip away?*

If you have children who seem to drift like this, it not time to wonder, it is time to pursue them. Sometimes they pull away because they just need some space. Other times it is to see if you will notice and seek them out. One son who did this needed some wind-down time from all the noise in our house. He did not want to bond during a round of cards or some other form of competition. He wanted some one-on-one time.

This is true when you have children who live in the shadow of a dominant older sibling or an attention-grabbing younger one. Often middle children are watchers and they want to know if you are watching for them ... make sure you are.

Live Wisely

Wisdom is the next virtue the older women are admonished to pass on. Living wisely means we understand that the choices we make today have the power to reach into our tomorrows and bring forth good or bad. Wise women weigh actions and reactions according to this principle. Wise women allow the truth of God's Word to have its way in every aspect of their lives.

Wise women understand time is something to be redeemed. There is no progress when each generation repeats the mistakes of the others. To live wisely we allow others to learn from our mistakes, which means we must first do likewise. No woman grows when she lives a life of blaming others and being trapped in her past. Wise women make mistakes, but they also learn from them. Because they learn from their failures, they offer others the opportunity to grow as well. (Pause for a minute and consider: what is a lesson you learned the hard way that you would not want your daughter to repeat?)

> ### Wise women allow the truth of God's Word to have its way in every aspect of their lives.

They don't always have to be right, because they have learned it is better to be rightly related. Some things seem monumental at the time but turn into nothing as the years wash over them. Living wisely is living with perspective and an understanding that life is truly made up of seasons and if you are wise, you will live fully present in your season.

So what is wisdom?

I believe wisdom is the intimate embrace of truth. I also believe wise women know how to make exchanges: when to let go and when to hold on. As daughters of God, we are to lay hold of His Word and His promises and let go of unforgiveness, bitterness, resentment, and the people and things we cannot change. This is just a short synopsis, but the impartation of wisdom is my entire reason for writing this book.

Be Pure

Purity is such a large topic that I want to devote several pages to it. Let's start by looking at the Word. Paul instructed Timothy as well as Titus:

> *Be an example to all believers in what you say, in the way you live, in your love, your faith, and your purity.* (1 TIMOTHY 4:12)

Paul's admonishment to Timothy lets us all know that even in our youth we are examples of purity, love, and faith by the way we live and speak. How much more should we who are mature model these attributes? I poured my heart and soul into a book on purity called *Kissed the Girls and Made Them Cry*, but in this chapter I want to briefly address the issue as it affects mothers and daughters by reviewing a classic Disney story.

Mirror, Mirror, on the Wall

Years ago when I was working on *Kissed the Girls and Made Them Cry*, I woke one morning with the words "Snow White" whispered in my ears. It was summer and I was up early so, as the rest of the house slept, I padded down to the basement to review my children's collection of fairy tales. But as I leafed through the different books, the story of Snow White was nowhere to be found.

The household was waking, so after feeding the guys, I slipped out and rented the Disney classic on video. As a child I had seen the movie in the theater and found it terrifying. (Okay, I also wept over Bambi!) Over forty years had passed since I had seen the original movie, so I thought surely it would not frighten me now. Oh, but I was wrong.

As you probably remember, there's a dark dressing chamber where a wicked queen daily assesses her beauty rank of "fairest of them all." But one day there is a crisis: her stepdaughter, Princess Snow White, displaces the evil seductress as the "fairest." Enraged, the queen looks out the window at her rival. Snow White is singing in a courtyard, totally unaware she just won a beauty pageant or of the pending danger. She is a princess waiting for a prince, and her song draws the attention of one. He peers over the wall and glimpses this royal daughter in rags and begins to answer her in song. The evil queen sees this interchange and determines Snow White will not marry. She knows that if Snow White becomes the prince's, she will be protected. The queen will have no chance of regaining the distinction of "fairest of them all." Then and there she decides the princess must die!

Short version of the remainder of the story: her death is ordered, but the princess escapes to the temporary safety of the cottage of the seven dwarves. The queen discovers she has been deceived and that Snow White is yet alive. The queen disguises herself and devises a plan involving a tempting and poisonous apple. Snow White is deceived, bites into the apple, and falls into a deathlike sleep of oblivion until the prince awakens her with a kiss.

As I watched this film, I heard the Spirit of God pose this question: "How long will the women of your generation be so captivated by their own images in the mirror that they refuse to turn their hearts to the daughters? The daughters have been driven from the shelter of home and have hid in the company of foolish men, hoping somehow a prince will find and rescue them."

We Have Lost Perspective

I began to shake with the realization...*It is true. We have lost our perspective.* Before any mothers are offended, understand I believe this movie reflects a spiritual battle. The spirit of this world is trying to separate mothers and daughters from their positions of strength. Arrested, I had an "aha" moment. Afterward, everywhere I turned I saw this tension in play. There appeared to be an incessant drive to focus the middle-aged women on the small, seductive world of self while daughters struggled seemingly alone with major life challenges.

The spirit of this world is trying to separate mothers and daughters from their positions of strength.

Please understand, I am not an advocate of women neglecting themselves to care for their daughters. But there seems to be a separation rather than a God-given connection. We are women who walk through an earthly life made up of seasons. Beauty and strength are to be found in each and every season, but we face vulnerability and weakness when we try to skip one season to enter another. Our strength similarly weakens if we strain for what is passed and neglect to give attention to what is before us. Seasoned women empower others to find their way.

Sadly, I've observed what would appear to be jealousy of the daughters' emerging beauty. It is as though mothers seek to diminish rather than celebrate it. These mothers seem to be at once critical of and competitive with their daughters. Alongside this group there are foolish mothers who appear almost to abandon their maternal role to embrace the role of girlfriend. (Picture the mom in *Mean Girls*.) I am not saying this is a majority problem, but it does seem to be a rising trend. When mothers abandon their role, a lot that was meant to be passed on to daughters is lost.

Daughters need mothers, not friends. Mothers do eventually become friends and confidants, but this transition normally happens when daughters are fully mature. Our young girls don't need more peers, they need people seasoned and wiser. So what is really happening here?

Somehow, through the neglect of her father and the absence of a true mother, Snow White has been reduced to a servant when she is in fact an heiress. Snow White is a glaring metaphor for our daughters today. God Himself promised,

> *Though your sins are like scarlet, I will make them as white as snow.*　　　(ISAIAH 1:18)

God's daughters can be referred to as beautiful, pure, and virginal, not because they have always lived perfectly but because the sacrifice of His Son has washed them clean. A royal, unstained righteousness has been bestowed on these princesses of promise. They are altogether lovely in His sight.

> **Snow White has been reduced to a servant when she is in fact an heiress.**

In contrast, whom does the wicked stepmother represent? This evil temptress is the polar opposite of the lovely Snow White. Seductively draped in a dark, gothic beauty, her form is all angles and edges. The demotion of Snow White and exaltation of the queen is strangely prophetic for today. Our culture declares, "Purity is weak and powerless. Why wait for a prince to find you? Use what you have and take what you want. Seduction and manipulation will bring you what you want...now!"

We glimpse a battle for the sexual purity of women on every level. This dark queen is a type and shadow of the spirit of this world. The very force that rages against our daughters rages against the mothers as well. She is controlling, intimidating, and seductive; she operates by cunning, not wisdom. Conversely, the daughters of heaven are powerful, influential, wise, gracious, and lovely.

Shared Strength

You see, God is doing something beautiful and amazing for His daughters young and old. The last thing the enemy of our souls wants is for the women of all ages to lend their strengths to each other. We should not resent the loveliness of the daughters but in contrast do all we can to preserve and prepare them for princes. As mothers and grandmothers we need to do all that is within our power so a generation of daughters recovers its noble position and destiny. If we have known regret because of bad choices we made with our sexuality, we need to position them to walk in something better.

The last thing the enemy of our souls wants is for the women of all ages to lend their strengths to each other.

It is time we used our lives to model a hope and a future for them, that they would inherit the promises of God's beauty in the area of intimacy, and not our shame and pain.

There has never been a time when the image, beauty, and sexual purity of women have been so vehemently attacked. Mothers and daughters alike must change the way they approach purity.

Mothers, do not be afraid to speak to your daughters. They desperately want to hear from you. Daughters, go to your mothers and tell them you need their insight and affirmation. If you are struggling, get the support you need.

Note: At this point, Titus 2 would have me address the keeping of the home. I feel this is so crucial to the entire aspect of nurture that I have spent the next chapter detailing some ways to create an atmosphere of a nurturing home no matter where you live. Then Paul's next charge "to do good" is also such a large subject that chapter 11 is dedicated to its elaboration. So here we'll press into the next Titus directive: submission.

The daughters of heaven are powerful, influential, wise, gracious, and lovely.

Be Submissive to Your Husband

Wives are encouraged to be submissive to their husbands. Please understand God never meant for women to be abused by this directive. Men are not to abuse their authority but use their position to cause women to flourish by laying down their lives for them. This is a charge for men to be good, loving, gracious, kind providers. A husband is to love his wife as Christ loved the church and as if she were his own body. We are to be cared for lovingly and tenderly. For the woman, submission is predominantly attached to treating her husband in a way that honors him and the position God entrusted him with.

Submission is not a mindless concession. Healthy submission asks questions, but it does not demean or question the authority of the husband. Allow me to explain. You can be submissive and question the wisdom of a choice, but it is not submissive to undermine the right of your husband to lead.

This is a messy subject often mishandled by the church. The man is not to dominate but to serve his wife through his leadership. The wife is not to make it difficult for her husband to lead but to lend her insight, strength, and support to him so he can lead even more effectively.

Submission is not enabling bad habits and unhealthy interaction. Submission is using your position wisely to bring out the best in your husband. You are not bringing out the best in your mate if you allow him to speak dishonorably to you. You can say something to the effect of "Honey, I want to work through this with you, but I can't allow you to talk to me this way. So let's take a break and cool off and then we can reconvene later."

Wives can disagree and still be submissive. You are not to put your brain on "pause." I am tired of hearing of wives who knew their husbands were in blatant disobedience to the Word of God or the laws of the land and yet they remained silent because they were "submissive." That is not submission, that is being party to destruction.

> *Healthy submission asks questions, but it does not demean or question the authority of the husband.*

You should never be silent when you see violations of truth, but offer your input in a way that it can be heard. It is all about the approach. You want to be heard? Say it the way you would want to hear it yourself. Incorporate love and respect and make an appeal to his godliness and the true heart of the matter.

Submission and honor are intimately intertwined. Dishonor is our cultural norm. It is quite possible that if there is not a dramatic shift in the concept of honor between men and women, it may be lost completely if the older women do not teach and train the younger.

John cannot even hear what I am saying if he feels he is being dishonored. I may have a valid point but it will be utterly lost in translation. Submission has the attitude, *I am for you, I am for us, I want to work with you, not undermine you.*

The opposite of submission is resistance, which means to work against someone or to adopt an opposing stance. A wife who is resistant and resentful causes her house to be divided. When we have homes that are unified in purpose, everyone within flourishes.

> *A wife who is resistant and resentful causes her house to be divided.*

Find the Best "Mother" Possible

As you work to live out the Titus directives, seek the training you need from older, more experienced women.

There was a time when John and I were in the throes of conflict and I went to a confidant. The only problem is that when you ask advice of a friend, she is often frustrated if you don't follow it. To be honest, I was venting more than I was seeking advice. After I spilled the whole story and the peer began to dispense advice, something strange happened.

I heard the Holy Spirit speaking in one ear as I listened to the counsel of my confidant with the other. She encouraged me to do what sounded both logical and constructive. But as she spoke I heard a distinct warning: "Do not listen unless you want what she has."

I suddenly realized I needed to connect with someone who was presently living where I wanted to go.

When I hung up the phone I made a list of what I wanted. I wanted a healthy, strong, love-filled marriage. I wanted to grow old with John in a home filled with laughter. I wanted to be constructive in the midst of conflict. I did not want to develop a jaded attitude toward men. I didn't want to be overly possessive of my sons when the time came for them to love other women. I wanted to be an amazing mother-in-law. I wanted to be true to myself.

The more I considered the advice of my friend, the more I realized her counsel would not position me for where I wanted to head. I would need to come up a few steps higher to see that happen.

Then I wondered whom could I speak with to gain that kind of insight and perspective. I figured out really quick that it was not going to be a peer. I needed someone older and wiser. In my case, I went to a grandmother. I ended up talking to a beautiful woman who had been married to her husband for close to thirty years. The truth is, he is her third husband, she had been married twice before. Her right to speak into my life was not framed by where she'd been, but by where she was presently. She had known hardship, made mistakes, and learned from them. And for three decades, she had built a life of love and beauty.

I challenge you to make a list of what you hope for—paint a picture of where you want to land—then find women who presently live where you want to go. Honor their years and enlist the older and wiser—the mothers and grandmothers—as your advisors.

Now we have reviewed all of the aspects of the Titus mandate. I challenge you to really study these for yourself. In the next chapter we will talk about some of the elements necessary to foster an environment that causes gifts to flourish.

10

Creating an Environment of Nurture

ENVIRONMENT (noun): The conditions that surround people and affect the way they live.

Recently I had the wonderful opportunity to be part of a conference that was so healing and empowering. Before a word was spoken, my heart was already open and tender. As the first song began, tears were in my eyes. It was not that the words spoken or the principles shared were foreign to me—they were not. It was the atmosphere or environment in which they were released. The difference was as drastic as planting seeds in the perfectly prepared soil and controlled climate of a greenhouse versus planting the same seed in frozen ground. The seed is good in both cases but only one environment will cause it to flourish.

Environment and atmospheres can work for or against the fostering of nurture. In this chapter we are going to explore some practical ways to create an environment that nurtures what God has placed inside of you and inside the lives of those you come alongside.

The Value of Rituals

Rituals can be amazingly good things. When my children were toddlers, our lives were anything but normal. John was traveling extensively and the boys and I tagged along. We would pack up our Honda Civic with practiced precision. In the backseat of our car were two matching Fisher Price car seats. Between these we wedged a suitcase to separate our two sons, Addison and Austin. This way they could not hit, scratch, or in any other way violate the person or property of each other. Armed with multiple hours of worship tapes, Psalty, and the Amazing Book series of children's stories, John and I bravely faced road trips that often exceeded ten hours in the car.

At the time I was pregnant with Alec, and every three hours I got out so I could stretch (this usually meant I circled our parked car a few times). And, of course, we all needed bathroom breaks!

We stayed in quite a variety of places back then. More often than not we overnighted in the homes of congregation members. We stayed in campers in the backyard and quite frequently we found ourselves in mobile homes. This meant very different levels of comfort and an ever-changing environment. Our schedule usually required very late nights and, more often than not, early mornings.

My boys handled the travel quite well because even though the setting was ever changing, I did not vary their bedtime routine. Every night I rocked and sang to them and when they were younger, I bathed them as well. You see, since they had been born they had enjoyed the same nightly ritual: first a relaxing bath, then a time of cuddling, play, reading, and singing. Even though there was no rocking chair I would sway back and forth with them and almost as though on cue, they would drift off to sleep. But if we were to violate this elaborate process, there would be screaming as overly tired children would retaliate with a vengeance.

I vividly remember John, in desperation, placing one of our sons in a car seat in the middle of the kitchen floor at a random house hoping it would make him think he was traveling in the car and cause him to wind down...*not!*

These rituals of comfort lent them a piece of home when on the road. The rituals were just normal things that mothers worldwide do each day that help children feel safe and rest, even in a strange place.

Mothers Create Comfort

Mothers have such an amazing ability to create simple cues of comfort for their children. They have the awesome responsibility to make intimate connections with their sons and daughters and one of the keys to seeing this happen is routine.

Mothers have such an amazing ability to create simple cues of comfort for their children.

Believe me, there were many nights when we returned to our motel room exhausted and completely spent. All I wanted to do was drop the children onto their double bed, sleeper sofa, or crib and dive into bed with John. But we owed it to them to give them the last look, the last song, the last story of the day. You see, they had just spent hours—and I do mean hours—in various nurseries or drooling on my lap on the front row of a protracted church service. (Why is it that the smaller the church, the longer the service?) They watched as Mom and Dad made time for everyone else, and now it was their turn. Kisses, songs, and caresses—nurture—needed to happen. The importance of their relationships with us needed to be intimately affirmed.

Then their anxieties would be arrested and their bodies relaxed so they could rest and awake with excitement for the next day. I have never regretted spending those fifteen minutes or more each night with my sons.

Now that my boys are older, hardly a night goes by when I do not brew some herbal tea and offer it to whoever wants its comfort. We gather around the table to play games or cuddle on the sofa and watch TV with our hands wrapped around warm mugs.

What are some of the things you can do to create an atmosphere of warmth? It might be something you can make special and elevate that you already do as routine.

Emotional Warmth = Nurture

As I write, it is the dead of winter. It almost seems like a joke for me to speak of warmth in my Colorado home. We have not experienced warmth for quite a while and as the month of February opens before me, I have the remnants of December's snow all about me. I sit at my computer in polar fleece socks, thermal pajamas, and a massive hot pink terry-cloth robe. I know this is far from a vision of loveliness. I am just desperately trying to keep warm in an environment of subzero temperatures! I am wondering how my plants will fare the harshness of this winter season. We have had both snow and cold in abundance before, but never for such a sustained period of time.

If life is to flourish, it must have warmth or at least the hope of it. Scriptures frequently use the analogy of agriculture to teach us about ourselves. Not all exposure to cold is wrong for plants; without the cold, how would we ever truly relish the warmth? As a former inhabitant of the Sunshine State of Florida, I learned that if the oranges did not experience cold, the fruit would not be sweet. Something in the blast of chill air causes the orange tree to release into its fruit sweetness the Florida heat and humidity fail to inspire.

If life is to flourish, it must have warmth.

In Colorado we have to create rather the opposite dynamic. We are heat-seeking inhabitants. In almost every room in my house you will find blankets of various shapes, textures, and colors. There are sporty polar fleeces, fake mink throws, and one from New Zealand that looks rather like the backside of a wooly mammoth. I want to be certain that both the guests and inhabitants of our home are warm.

My obsession has become a bit of a hindrance to John. I love to sleep beneath a mound of layers. I love to feel safely cocooned in mantles of warmth, but John does not like all this weight on him. I usually wake buried by both his portion of the blankets and my own. Tia, our Yorkie, is often caught in the shuffle of blankets as well and most mornings I have to unearth her from a heap of covers.

The truth is, it is hard to relax and unwind when you are cold. All your body's energy is being utilized to recover the lost warmth. We were created for warmth, but ever since our naked revelation in the garden we have had to garner warmth from our surroundings. We build homes for shelter from the elements of nature, wear coats to maintain our body heat, rest in bed with comforters piled high, ever striking for the balance between warm and hot, cold and comfortable.

But warmth can be cultivated in more than outward ways. Warmth can be conveyed in a smile, a touch, a gift, a meal eaten together, and the beauty of our environment. Emotional warmth is an integral part of *nurture*.

Okay, let me step back a minute. I live with five men and my house is not beautiful...it is warm and functional and in some places, almost indestructible. When my boys and their friends come in, they can approach the sofa without fear—not because it is dirty already, but because everything on it is machine washable.

> *Warmth can be conveyed in a smile, a touch, a gift, a meal eaten together, and the beauty of our environment.*

Therefore, warmth is captured not only in terms of temperature; it is conveyed in an environment that invites others to enter and be comfortable. At my house the vibe is "Come in and play—we want to beat you at a game! And when we are done playing, we will eat!"

What rituals do you have in your life or family? (This may be something you are doing, but you were unaware you were creating rituals.) What rituals help you feel comforted and loved that you could use with others? If there are no rituals in place, what rituals would you like to create? An example may be: I want to have herbal tea each night with my daughter as we cuddle in her bed. Or if you are in need of self-comfort: I will have herbal tea and read a little each night before I go to bed.

Food and Laughter

In my opinion, you can never have too much of either of these in a home. Yes, you can eat too much but it is incredibly nurturing to know that if you are hungry, there is always something good to eat.

To my shame I used to be really stingy with my children and husband with food. I was almost prohibitive about it. I expected everyone else to be hungry only when I was, and I fed John the same size portion as me. There was never anything *fun* to eat in my house—there was only the healthy. My children began to sneak junk food into their rooms and they were always trying to negotiate trades with their organic lunches.

Healthy is good and important, but joy and laughter should be part of eating, and some how I had completely eliminated that portion.

How joyful are those who fear the LORD—all who follow his ways! You will enjoy the fruit of your labor. How joyful and prosperous you will be! Your wife will be like a fruitful grapevine, flourishing within your home. Your children will be like vigorous young olive trees as they sit around your table. That is the LORD's blessing for those who fear him. (PSALM 128:1–4)

People who truly fear the Lord are not grumpy—they are happy. When they gather at the table, they eat and enjoy God's goodness.

Even if the portions of food are small, they seem larger when presented with laughter rather than stinginess. I am all about allowing big loaves of bread, plates of olive oil, and pots of pasta to flesh out a meal. So be generous and enjoy!

People who truly fear the Lord are not grumpy— they are happy.

Laughter is medicine for the body and soul. Years ago, while John was videotaping a promo for his book *The Bait of Satan* in our small home, I was trying to keep children simultaneously entertained and quiet. Laughter kept escaping from the room we were in and the crew had to keep reshooting the segment. Finally I piled all the kids into the car and tossed a quick apology to the director.

The essence of his reply remains with me today: "The laughter of children in your home is one of the greatest blessings you'll ever know. Let them laugh. Laugh with them." Far too often we mothers are too bogged down with the mundane to experience the magic in our lives. Laugh while you eat!

As you continue building a nurturing ambience, ask yourself: *What foods am I comfortable and confident serving my family or friends? Am I generous with food or stingy? How can I get more laughter into my life and home?*

Lighting and Atmosphere as Nurture

Here are some other supereasy ways to create an environment that nurtures. This is rather straightforward: lighting should be appropriate for what you are doing. If it is a place of rest, the lighting should be soft. If it is a place for study and focus, then the lighting should be bright enough so everything is clear. If you are eating, it should be warm, not overly bright, so everyone relaxes. (Leftovers look better dimly lit.) I have found we all wind down when the lights are dimmer. I am sure it is a natural human response: as the light levels drop, we all switch into rest-and-connect mode.

The atmosphere should feel light as well. Dim is not to be mistaken for dismal. We have all sensed an ambience that feels hopeless and heavy. As women, we can steward the atmosphere of our homes, apartments, or dorm rooms. I find that uplifting music is the quickest way to lighten or shift a mood. I have music on almost perpetually.

Other times you have to take it to the next level and arrest the heaviness through prayer. Times of prayer are the most effective when you know who you are in Christ and what you need to address in the atmosphere. If you have turned up the music and lights, and the atmosphere still feels heavy, then it needs to be addressed in the Spirit.

> ### *Times of prayer are the most effective when you know who you are in Christ.*

Very real forces stand against us. Do not allow this to frighten you—there is no reason it should. But when there is an oppressive presence, address it in prayer and tell it to lift.

Smaller Spaces Are Good

Bigger is not always the best option. We have lived in five different houses in our twenty-five years of marriage and in each we found our family loves to gather in intimate spaces.

In one of our houses we had a grand entrance with a formal living and dining area. Guess what—we never used them! We would almost hurry through those high-ceilinged, formal areas to get to where we really wanted to go.

Everyone always congregates in the areas that are comfortable and inviting. Our kitchen and eating nook are overrun with teenage friends and family members. This is the place where we bump into each other while pasta is strained and tomatoes are cut. Last night my twelve-year-old and I sat on the kitchen floor in front of the sink as we sipped tea and worked on his history homework. There is something safe about close quarters when the inhabitants feel loved.

When creating an atmosphere of nurture, you need a space you can fill without anyone feeling isolated. I would rather speak to a jam-packed room of two hundred women than five hundred women spread out in a sanctuary or venue that holds a thousand. The feeling is completely different. In the larger but semi-empty venue, the women don't know where to sit. I don't know where to look, and we all feel so disconnected.

Do you assume that you need a big house to entertain effectively—to offer comfort and friendship to others? Do you hesitate to invite people over because you think your house is too small or too modest in décor? Don't stop yourself—invite them in. People remember the warmth of a home more than its scale.

If you are considering opening your home and life to others, don't think it has to be big to be effective.

Spreading Out

There is a time and place to enlarge. When a plant has outgrown its pot, it is in danger of becoming root-bound. In the past I have made the mistake of just lifting the plant from its small, confining pot and plopping the pot-shaped tangle of roots and soil into a larger container or opening in the earth—with disastrous results.

The tangle of roots must be broken apart. If we don't do this, the roots do not "realize" they have been transferred to a larger container and they continue in their present growth pattern. Plants I transplanted without first detangling the roots were shrunken or dead a year later. When I lifted them from the soil their roots looked the same as when I had planted them a year previous.

To successfully transplant, the network of roots has to be gently expanded so that it no longer mimics the shape of the pot. The roots must be directed outward in all directions. I was always afraid to do this—I didn't want to rip up too many of the roots in the process. But it is a necessary evil.

Now we're going to switch our focus to nurture in the house of God because this is one container that needs to enlarge. So how does this apply to the idea of nurture and daughters in the house of God? Well, when we review most of our current church culture and its women's ministry, we soon discover the majority of women's ministry is root-bound. Not to sound perverse, but sometimes I fear the dynamics are a bit inbred as well. It is always the same women doing the same things; we need fresh ideas and young blood. We build bigger church buildings but too often fail to foster the nurture and heart of the house. We simply repot the confined in a bigger pot and never release the tangled roots. I have no doubt that women of all ages capture a portion of the heart of God for His house, but we gather the women without ever extending the reach of their roots. At the close of the meeting we send them out the door with the admonishment: "Go home and be good and nice moms and daughters." That is all well and fine, but the world is bigger than we are and good and nice are just not going to cut it anymore. There are lots of hurting people outside our walls.

> ### We build bigger church buildings but too often fail to foster the nurture and heart of the house.

The church must extend its reach and mind-set beyond the building borders. As I travel I find a lot of women's ministry is just silly. I fear too much time is spent telling women what they can't do rather than telling them what they can do. Daughters, you can do whatever God has placed in your heart!

> *I can do everything through Christ, who gives me strength.*
> (PHILIPPIANS 4:13)

God does not exempt you from this promise because you are His daughter. The verse does not say "Men can do all things through Christ, but the women are weak so let them drink tea." Having tea together is great and relaxing. But it can be somewhat less than life-changing if we are not around the table celebrating and brainstorming how each of us can change the dynamics of our world.

You have a sphere of influence to steward and each year that sphere should enlarge. Why? You will never be satisfied if you are not a world-changer. Yes, it starts at home but it doesn't end there—it should reach far beyond it.

If we think small, then next year we will all show up once again just to listen and hear and go away nice and alone again. We can't empower others to do what we haven't done ourselves. Ask yourself: *Am I being stretched to live what I learn? What is one thing I can do to break apart my roots and expand my life and reach?*

You will never be satisfied if you are not a world-changer.

I am tired of being nice.... I want my roots spread out and my heart broken so that my world and influence are enlarged. If we are sufficiently dislodged and stretched before transplanting, we will actually grow into the likeness of what we have heard and seen. We will be solid and stronger when our reach is extended and roots untangled. If not, we will keep moving from meeting to meeting but never truly grow.

They are the kind who work their way into people's homes and win the confidence of vulnerable women who are burdened with the guilt of sin and controlled by various desires. (Such women are forever following new teachings, but they are never able to understand the truth.) (2 TIMOTHY 3:6–7)

Why are they "forever following new teachings"? Is it because they have yet to walk in the old teachings? They hear, but they fail to do. This dangerous dynamic is the breeding ground of deception. The old teachings do not seem to be enough for their purposeless lives, so they are always looking for something new. They may constantly be transplanted from one house to another and one conference to another, but because their root system is dwarfed they fail to truly flourish.

God is always about doing a new thing, but it comes by following the old teaching of what it means to be godly and walk in His power and might.

If we get together but are never mobilized, then a year later Sister So-and-So is still in the same bondage as she was at the last retreat. Are we afraid of new soil? Too often we hold an event but then we fail to empower the attendees to do something with what they learned. Our group may grow, but is anyone's life changed in a practical, consistent way?

Manners

I know this seems a major segue, but no one will get what she needs at our conferences, churches, or homes if greeted with rudeness. Manners are an important aspect of nurture. Practicing good etiquette shows respect for the people around you and honors their presence. It creates an atmosphere for positive interaction and encouragement.

My mother worked hard to instill far more etiquette and manners than I have managed to retain. I am now in the process of recovering what I tossed aside as outdated and unnecessary in our rather uncivil world.

I am not sure how it happened, but the Christian culture seems to project a vibe saying that it is acceptable, if not quite possibly at times spiritual, to be rude. Before you get defensive, I hope you will hear me out with this. Let's begin by laying a ground rule: it is never becoming for anyone, least of all Christian women, to be rude. Being a daughter of heaven does not give you a license to be rude on Earth. We are not some elite group of forgiven snobs...we are Earth's servants. If anything we have to be kinder, gentler, and politer than any other daughters who walk the earth.

> ### Being a daughter of heaven does not give you a license to be rude on Earth.

Yet in my travels I have met more rude Christian women than I could even dare to recount. Mind you, they are not the sweet ones hosting me. They are usually Christian women who do not know another Christian is watching. These are the women who are rude in restaurants, sisters who are rude in airports, daughters behaving badly at hairdressers' shops and dentist offices. They are usually well behaved at the conferences, but even that is not guaranteed.

Admittedly, at times I, too, have been a rude Christian woman. So please understand I write this chapter with the hope that none of us will remain that way. Let's all let go of any indefensible behavior in the past and recapture the art of being gracious.

Some Definitions

Before we go on to some telling examples, let's define some terms.

Manners and etiquette are often linked but they are not same.

ETIQUETTE (noun): Comes from the French word for "ticket," which at one time was used to outline the proper path or course for the French nobility to follow as they navigated the gardens of Versailles.[1]

Let's simplify this for our use and declare etiquette *the noble approach to the course of life*. Etiquette is referred to as the *language of manners*. Good etiquette should govern our behavior in every interaction and help people get along.

For our definition of manners there is no finer source than Emily Post: "Manners are made up of trivialities of deportment which can be easily learned if one does not happen to know them; manner is personality—the outward manifestation of one's innate character and attitude toward life."

Our outward manners display or reveal our inner character. The basis for good manners is respect, consideration, and kindness to our fellow inhabitants of Earth. Do you see why these are important dynamics to recover?

> *For God was in Christ, reconciling the world to himself, no longer counting people's sins against them. And he gave us this wonderful message of reconciliation. So we are Christ's ambassadors; God is making his appeal through us. We speak for Christ when we plead, "Come back to God!"*
>
> (2 CORINTHIANS 5:19–20)

AMBASSADOR (noun): 1. a diplomatic official of the highest rank sent by one country as its long-term representative to another. 2. an official representative of an organization or movement.[2]

In light of these definitions, we had better get with the program. We are not merely representing ourselves to the world around us, we represent the kingdom of heaven and the cause of Christ. It is completely inappropriate for us to behave in a rude or ignorant manner.

> **We represent the kingdom of heaven and the cause of Christ.**

Etiquette Specifics

Here are some basic etiquette ideas to help you foster an environment of nurture.

Introduction etiquette. Take the time to be sure everyone is introduced and included. You can do this even if you are not the host. Wait a moment or two for the host or hostess to do it, but if he or she doesn't, then you facilitate it. If you find yourself in a group and no one has introduced you, don't get offended. Introduce yourself. Look each person in the eye, extend your hand, and say, "Hello, my name is. . . ." This sets everyone at ease. They will know you want to meet them and learn their names. It is always more comfortable when everyone present knows each other's name. If you forget a name, then just be honest and ask someone.

Restaurant etiquette. If you are dealing with someone involved in the service industry, whenever possible use his or her name. If a waitress comes to take your order, look at her name tag, and then say, "Hi, Shannon. I would love to order the. . . ." Again, this communicates that you see her as an individual with a name.

If you are given a wine list and you will not be drinking, don't make the big Christian announcement, "We don't drink!" This makes it awkward for everyone, and no one asked if you drink. If the wine list is offered, say something like, "Thank you, but we will not need that tonight." Remember, you're always striving to create an atmosphere of nurture—and graciously interacting with your server is part of that.

Nothing more needs to be said. It is no different from choosing not to order an appetizer. You do not need to declare your lack of alcohol consumption to the world. The hostess is just trying to serve you. She is not questioning your righteousness!

At the end of the meal, tip according to the service rendered. A few dollars is not a lot to you, but again, it speaks volumes to those who serve you. If the service was bad or if you are going to be cheap, for goodness' sake, don't leave a tract! (Okay, can you tell I used to be a waitress? It is very hard work.)

Ministry etiquette. If you are speaking at a conference where there are other speakers, be sure to add value to them. Say things like, "I know God is going to build in each session and you don't want to miss the next one with. . . ."

This will do wonders to put the women in attendance and put the other speaker at ease. Remember, you are there to do a conference with them! You are not there to outpreach or compete with them for product sales. You are there together to build the lives of those in attendance.

Be respectful of your time limits. The amount of time you go over is the time you take from other speakers. Always confirm with the conference host exactly how much time she wants you to take and then stick with it. Do not ask her in front of the crowd if you can go longer—it is too hard for her to say no, so she will say yes. But she will not really mean it and she might resent it. You can take the extra fifteen minutes but you may never be asked back.

Be polite to the people who are hosting you. They look up to you and more likely than not have put in both labor and time to see you there and comfortable.

If you are hosting a minister, do not talk nonstop to the speaker on his or her way to service. Often this is a time when the speaker is still listening to God about the service, so be sensitive. If he or she talks then you can respond, but don't start spilling out your life calling or story on the way to the service. Ministers are very empathetic people and they will feel pressured to fix what you are talking about rather than focus on what God is whispering in that moment. God can anoint them to speak into your life, but let it happen naturally.

> *One day I was … saying a record number of stupid things and a good, dear friend reminded me that I could feel free not to talk.*

No matter who you are, don't name-drop or talk about yourself nonstop. Instead, ask questions so you can reach into the lives of others.

One day I was particularly tired and saying a record number of stupid things and a good, dear friend reminded me that I could feel free *not* to talk. Sometimes it is just better to listen until you really know the person you are with.

Be a Generous Daughter, Not a Diva

Look with me at Proverbs 18:16:

A man's gift makes room for him. (NKJV)

The New Living Translation says it this way:

Giving a gift can open doors; it gives access to important people!

Divas flip this verse and project an attitude that says, "I am the gifted, make room for me!" Just because you are a talented singer, speaker, or successful entrepreneur, it does not give you the license to be rude. Just because you are anointed, you do not have the right to act superior. Maybe that works in the economy of Hollywood, but it is certainly a no-no in God's kingdom. The beautiful, gifted daughters I have had the privilege of knowing are humble and gracious no matter whom they are speaking with.

Your gift or talent is to be presented to others even before any doors are opened to you. Elisha was faithfully plowing his father's field when Elijah called him to serve. This means you should already be faithfully administrating and releasing the gift even before it makes room or opens any doors for you.

If your gift is singing, you should already be singing. If your gift is teaching or speaking, you should share your talent with others. If your gift is giving, then be generous. Ask yourself: *Am I generous with what I have? Do I faithfully give now or am I waiting for a door of opportunity to open?* Be found faithfully distributing the gift you have within. This is a primary way to nurture others.

Be found faithfully distributing the gift you have within.

If you are interested in learning more on manners, there are some amazing online resources you can check out—there are even some really fun tests so you can evaluate how skilled you are with manners. If you make it your goal to adjust just one habit a week, you will be well on your way to becoming a full-fledged ambassador.

I understand this chapter has been more of a compilation of practicalities than the other chapters. I want you to experience and extend nurture on every level so that your life is surrounded with strength and beauty.

11

The Wail That Swallowed My Life

WAIL (verb): To express pain, grief, or misery in a long, mournful cry.[1]

There have been two incidents in my existence when weeping and wailing changed my life. Daughters, please understand I am not referring to whining, which we all know is just plain annoying. Whining, as any mother can tell you, is completely self-focused and therefore void of any life-changing power because nothing changes when we are busy feeling sorry for ourselves.

No, I speak of a crying of another kind—wailing and weeping. For those of you who have never experienced this, allow me to describe the difference between a wail and a good old-fashioned cry. A wail comes from deep within. It cannot be manufactured, for it occurs when spirit and flesh collide and an utterance is released before you are even aware of what has happened. It is as though a portal of compassion is opened and you find yourself sucked into a black hole of despair that no earthly words can describe. The confrontation is so profound it cannot be contained.

This release may happen in response to devastating news. Natural disasters, the death of a loved one or leader may elicit a wail from those reeling in shock or grief. It can be birthed while deep in intercessory prayer. This dynamic may occur while you are crying out in repentance on a personal or corporate level. No matter what evokes or inspires the wail, it is not an everyday occurrence. It is possible wailing may happen only once in a lifetime, but if it has ever happened to you—you know it. It is almost a birth of something too painful to contain in our human form, the expression of something otherwise unutterable.

My First Wail

My first full-fledged wail occurred quite unexpectedly, while I was folding laundry. I was wrapping up a long day and while my two preschool sons were upstairs preparing for bed, I seized the opportunity to fold some of the ever-present laundry. I plopped down on the floor and dumped the basket of clean clothes out before me. I am not a big fan of folding clothes in front of the TV because what takes me five minutes in the laundry room can take up to a half an hour with the TV on. But I was tired and needed to hear another adult voice in my home. (Yes, John was on yet another long trip.)

I flipped hurriedly through the various news channels when a program showing a baby in utero caught my attention. As I'd recently been made a mother again by the birth of a second son, I was intrigued by the whole concept of a window to the world of the unborn. I had not had a sonogram with my first son, but the procedure had become routine by the time I was pregnant with my second.

The technology had still been a bit blurry, though, and I spent almost the entire time of my sonogram trying to get the technician to explain what I was actually seeing. I was so confused as I lay there with a gel-coated belly straining to see the monitor. For some reason I just was not seeing things as clearly as the technician did. "That's a head! Oh, I thought that was a stomach." As soon as I would gain somewhat of a perspective, the technician would switch to another image. I was completely confused by the experience...was my baby supposed to look like that?

All I knew for certain when I left was that I was having another healthy son. I was given a few black-and-white grainy prints, one that depicted my son (who rather looked like an alien) sucking his thumb. When I showed these images to his soon-to-be big brother, "Addison, here is your baby brother!" he shook his head and appeared disturbed.

In contrast with my blurred experience, the TV images were much more distinct. The form and outline of the baby were clearly visible. I recognized the head and even the baby's features were distinguishable. It was beautiful. I watched as the little life floated and moved fluidly in its watery home. Intrigued, I kept watching, assuming it was a health documentary. Nothing prepared me for what I saw next.

It was an abortion captured from the vantage point of an infant. I watched in horror as the translucent being tried to avoid the instrument that had quite suddenly invaded its sanctuary. The baby jerked away but there was nowhere to hide. It flitted this way and that, and then the instrument hit its mark. I watched as the formerly placid fetus appeared to scream in pain. The unconscious mother had reacted when her uterus was breached as well, but neither her audible cry or the fetus' silent one stopped the process. The infant was neatly and efficiently cut into manageable pieces so it could be vacuumed out.

That was when I heard the wail. Any lack of sound on the baby's part was certainly made up for by me. It was strange, but I realized almost after the fact that I was the one giving voice to what I heard. I never imagined I could make such a noise. Time seemed suspended. I was no longer watching the program because I was rocking back and forth, wailing. My two sons came running from upstairs only to find their mother doubled over in the midst of toddler laundry. Unsure of what was going on, they began to pat me, saying, "Mommy, are you okay? What's wrong?"

I never imagined I could make such a noise.

They threw their warm, soft arms around me as their faces pressed nearer, but I was undone. They kept vigil as I wept into the carpet. The wail had passed and left a river of tears in its wake. I was crying out for forgiveness—begging forgiveness for our nation, for this life lost, for my selfish attitude. I was sorry that I had said to John, "No more children." If babies were unwanted and dying at the hands of their mothers, then I would willingly give life to the ones destined for me.

When the storm was over, I felt completely emptied of myself.

As I came to myself, I found my second son asking, "Okay? Okay?" as he peered intently into my eyes. I hugged them both and left the unfolded laundry on the floor as I ushered them both upstairs for an extralong session of bedtime stories and lullabies.

In less than a month, my life was enlarged. I actually became pregnant with my beautiful third son on my eighth wedding anniversary. (We like to say he was an anniversary present from God.) In less than a year, Joshua Alexander was born. He has been a joy boy since the moment we laid eyes on him. His name has significance (as all names do!): *Joshua* declares "Jehovah is salvation" and *Alexander* means "defender of mankind." I cannot imagine our family without the light of his existence. Three years later our fourth son, Arden Christopher, graced our lives: *Arden* for "fiery and determined" and *Christopher* for "anointed one." Again, life without him is unimaginable. He is such a gift from heaven, so tender and true.

So what actually happened when I wailed? Well, obviously it wasn't the wailing that got me pregnant. It did not open the womb of my body—it opened the womb of my life. Somehow my capacity to live outside myself was awakened and my life was enlarged. Albert Einstein said, "A person starts to live when he can live outside himself."

I really believe that until then, I was merely surviving. You see, two children and a husband who traveled full-time were doable for me. My life was manageable and comfortable. Two children worked in our small house. Two children worked with our small salary. Two children made sense because we had no medical insurance. The idea of more than two pushed me completely out of my comfort zone.

A person starts to live when he can live outside himself.

Please don't imagine that I think everyone needs to have more children. I am not recommending everyone or anyone makes my experience her own. I am merely using an example of what happened in my life. It was something God asked of me in that moment.

You see, I had set up little boundaries and parameters around my life to keep things nice, safe, and orderly, and God was getting ready to expand my borders on every front—by enlarging my family and thus enlarging my heart and life. With two children I could trifold all the underwear and bleach all the grout. With two children I could maintain what I had. But the truth is none of us were ~~created~~ for maintenance, we were made for expansion. Daughter of the Most High, God wants to enlarge the life of each and every one us. He wants to push us out over the brink of what we can control in our own abilities and strength and position us to realize the lives He has for us outside our neat and tidy packages.

In short, He wants us to—as mentioned in the last chapter—reach beyond and extend our roots, even when it complicates our lives.

My Second Wail

The second wail occurred on an evening I was nursing my third son, Alec, while watching TV. I had turned it on as I walked by it, climbed onto the bed, and was well into the nursing process when I realized the remote was not responding to my commands. It was obvious I would need to resign myself to whatever programs appeared on this designated channel for the next thirty minutes. Again, I was not prepared for what was coming.

Desolate and starving children in Africa floated across my screen as a relief program kicked in full force. I was so uncomfortable I tried again to switch channels by whacking the remote and trying out different angles. The truth is, what I saw frightened me. I wanted to help others but the needs seemed too overwhelming. Try as I might, though, the TV would not switch stations.

The story became more focused as two women approached an emaciated mother who listlessly cradled in her frail arms a severely malnourished child. The little one was gasping as it struggled to breathe, its distorted body straining with great effort just to live another moment. Though this mother had walked many miles, traveling night and day, they had come too late to the feeding station. This little one no longer possessed the strength to take in and assimilate nourishment.

I watched as a South African woman gently lifted the child from its mother's arms and began to address the viewers. All three women gathered near as though by encircling this baby they might keep it from death, while flies buzzed about them and troubled the child's mouth and eyes.

The contrast was so poignant. Here I was, propped up by pillows atop my comfortable bed under a ceiling fan in my air-conditioned house, freely nursing my son, while the mother in Africa could not sustain the life of hers. Her breasts were not full like mine. Nor were they merely empty—they were shriveled. I had more milk than my son could consume, as the child now sleeping at my breast testified. I looked down and saw the peaceful contentment on his face. He was satiated even as this child of Africa starved.

Then the struggle was over and the child of Africa breathed no more. The tiny life was gone from this savage land where mothers beat at the wind to sustain the life of their infants. The mother did not even seem immediately to react. It was just another weight added to the shoulders that had already borne far too much sorrow and pain. It was almost an act of resignation, a yielding once again to the death and destruction that ravaged her land.

She had spent her last hope and it had not been enough.

But I reacted. The two white women who flanked her cried as I began to wail. I was again utterly overcome. This mother who had nothing would have given anything to save the life of this little one. As far as I could tell this child was all the wealth she possessed in the world and now this fragile life was swept away. She had spent her last hope and it had not been enough.

In comparison, I had so much and was really doing nothing. In that moment, the way I saw my financial position shifted. In that season, I was a young, stay-at-home mother with three preschool children on a very tight budget. Each paycheck I was given envelopes with cash in them: one held my allotment for gas, another contained my grocery budget, and then there was an envelope for miscellaneous expenses that cropped up or to cover overages in the other budgeted areas. And when the cash was gone . . . it was gone.

John had recently resigned his youth pastor position and was traveling full-time and we believed God for every cent that came into our house. We shared one car. Sometimes I felt rather poor when I looked at other families, but in contrast with this mother in Africa, I was actually rich!

When this realization hit me, my focus changed. I no longer saw my life and finances in terms of what I didn't have. I saw what I had. I knew it wasn't a lot, but I had so much more than her! I was going to give so more babies would not die.

We should give in response to the leading of the Holy Spirit, but we should never be compelled to give in response to another person's greed.

I did something immediately. I laid aside the sleeping baby and called my boys together and announced that as a family, we were going to do something to help those children. We set a minimum amount right then and there. Have you ever noticed how important this is? Usually, if I do not respond right away, I reason it away. Understand, I am not talking about giving in response to someone's demand but about obedience to the Holy Spirit's prompting. We should give in response to need, we should give in response to the leading of the Holy Spirit, but we should never be compelled to give in response to another person's greed.

Interestingly enough, even though my household budget had just gotten a bit tighter, I suddenly felt enlarged and generous. This stay-home mother suddenly had her life tied to something bigger, something nobler than her everyday world of housework and diapers. I had always wanted to travel overseas and tangibly do something to help others—and in that moment, I was. Something had shifted in the spirit as seeds were being planted in the best soil ever.

The Reward of Giving

> *If you help the poor, you are lending to the LORD—and he will repay you!* (PROVERBS 19:17)

Don't you love the exclamation mark in this verse? God is excited about this. When you give to those who can never repay you, God provides recompense for the money you lend Him.

There is a special reward reserved for us when we exhibit child-of-God-type behavior.

There is a special reward reserved for us when we exhibit child-of-God-type behavior. God is a giver and so likewise we should give. We are each blessed to be a blessing. What comes to our hands becomes dusty and stagnant when it stops with us. Yes, some of the blessing is for us to keep, some is for us to multiply, some is for us to pass on, and some is to be given away—but all is ours only to steward. There is ultimately no ownership for the daughter of God.

With this promise there is a warning as well:

The sin of your sister Sodom was this: She lived with her
daughters in the lap of luxury—proud, gluttonous, and lazy.
They ignored the oppressed and the poor. They put on airs
and lived obscene lives. And you know what happened: I did
away with them.　　　　　(EZEKIEL 16:49–50 THE MESSAGE)

Once our awareness is awakened, we are empowered to respond. I didn't send something only that one time to ease my conscience. We contributed to the organization monthly. Our giving started small, but over time it grew and expanded!

She extends a helping hand to the poor and opens her arms
to the needy.　　　　　(PROVERBS 31:20)

From this verse we see that it is a stretch or extension of ourselves to help the poor. I love the idea of a woman reaching out beyond her home to lift the lives of others. It is time for God's daughters to open their arms to the needy and extend assistance to the poor. Each of us can make a small difference and collectively the effect will be vast.

We began to sow through Messenger International. At the time of this writing (fourteen years later), we are still privileged to support this organization. Over the years our financial support grew into a relational connection that has enlarged our lives and ministries.

A Dream Seed Grows

Years later, the consistent seed caused my life dream to come true. First John traveled to Angola and was part of the on-site feeding teams we had supported for years. Seven years later, I was invited to travel overseas as well. I had just returned from the Philippines. After traveling all night, I had landed in Denver around 2:30 in the morning, slept a few short hours, got up, hugged all my boys, and sent them off to school. During my trip to the Philippines I had been reminded of just how much I loved the Asian women. I felt my heart would burst with love for them when suddenly John's office phone rang. It was one of the leaders from the relief organization calling. He shared how he knew how I had always wanted to go on a trip to Africa and was unable to go when they had invited John.

I listened with my heart pounding. Africa was not possible, but would I be interested in going to Cambodia? Yes! I blurted out even before he had the chance to give me the dates. Somehow the call was already in my heart before I received it. He gave me the dates and the option of asking John, but I knew I was already there! I had to go. I was part of releasing something that was welling up within me— something that had been slowly but surely growing ever since the day I nursed Alec and witnessed the baby dying. I had responded then, and now it was time I compelled others to respond as well.

> *But I had to speak for those who had no voice, just as you will someday speak for those who cannot.*

It was a life-changing trip. I walked among the orphans and again wept, I touched dirty children and did not recoil, I smelled things I do not know how to describe, I witnessed first-hand man's inhumanity to man. This time I was on the other side of the glass wall, urging mothers just like me that they could in fact make a difference. It was both humbling and empowering. Never had I felt so inadequate to communicate what I saw. At times my words failed me and I just cried. But I had to speak for those who had no voice, just as you must speak for those who cannot.

Constructive Compassion

You see, that second wail opened up a new portal in my life. It released constructive compassion, which includes follow-through. Hurting humanity has always moved me, but I did not always move beyond the tears and questioning to actually do something. To be quite honest, I am not sure I knew how to move beyond the sadness. When I saw the hopeless...I felt paralyzed and inadequate.

Daughters, witnessing people in pain is uncomfortable. Starving children should make us at least fidget. But fidgeting and shedding tears are not enough if you don't actually do something with the pain that has been awakened.

You may ask, *What can I do?* Far more than you know. Each one of us has a circle of influence in our world and during our short season on this earth, we possess the power to effect change. We live in a world that is hurting, but we steward an answer. This earth is full to overflowing with needs and pain. But there are just as many ways and individuals crafted to meet and heal them. Your giving and serving may start small, but they will always end up with an impact that is big if you are consistent.

> *But if anyone has this world's goods (resources for sustaining life) and sees his brother and fellow believer in need, yet closes his heart of compassion against him, how can the love of God live and remain in him?* (1 JOHN 3:17 AMP)

If we see needs and do not respond, a window in our hearts closes. A little less light and fresh air are granted entrance and a little more shadow creeps in. Please understand, I know you cannot respond to every need you see in a financial way, nor should you. But there are many needs we *can* respond to—and it's time to do so.

Nothing given is ever lost. It is just relocated.

When we commit to move beyond turning away or just feeling saddened, somehow the Holy Spirit causes us to "see" or take special notice of the needs we have the power to respond to. Some of these needs will require the giving of this world's goods, as a portion of what is in our hands or household is transferred into theirs.

Nothing given is ever lost. It is just relocated. The "world's goods" refers to the produce or substance of the good of this earth that we move from one place to another. Somehow this earthly transfer works a spiritual transformation. The temporal redistribution releases the human heart to experience compassion and nurture that is constructive.

It Starts in the Heart

My little children, let us not love in word or in tongue, but in deed and in truth. And by this we know that we are of the truth, and shall assure our hearts before Him.

(1 JOHN 3:18–19 NKJV)

Notice how it always comes back to an issue of the heart. If the heart is healthy, then healthy responses happen. We are able to "see" and the discernment we need is there for us. But if the heart is unhealthy, our ability to "see" or discern correctly is thwarted and our ability to move in with compassion is blocked or shut down.

The good news is that if we have the power to close our hearts by not responding, it stands to reason we can open our hearts by responding. The crusty, distrustful, and jaded then can be childlike and compassionate again. Jesus acted constantly with constructive compassion. He was "moved with compassion" and taught in Mark 6:34 (NKJV), moved with compassion and performed the miracle of the loaves and fishes in Mark 8:2, moved with compassion over a weeping mother who had lost her son and raised the dead in Luke 7:13, was compassionate to "those who are ignorant and going astray" in Hebrews 5:2 (NKJV) and interceded for their weaknesses. If one man, Jesus the Christ, who was filled with the Spirit of the Most High God, could touch so many by allowing His heart to be moved with compassion by pain, what could happen if a mighty host of His beautiful daughters likewise allowed compassion to move them? He was moved by compassion so He could be an answer and our passion.

Steward Well Your Gift

There are strangers who need a smile and a kind word. There are friends who need encouragement. There are organizations in need of volunteers. There are charities that depend on your faithful support. There are those who have never heard the truth of the gospel who need you not only to preach it but to demonstrate it in a viable, tangible way.

> *Here is the exciting part: no matter what place you find yourself in, there is always someone you can give to!*

You may feel in need yourself right now. But here is the exciting part: no matter what place you find yourself in, there is always someone you can give to! There is someone hurting out there who needs just what you have. You may argue you have nothing, but that is just not true. As long as we have breath there remains something of value in our lives that can be contributed to others—even if it is only to use our lives as illustrations of what not to do.

Here is just a small example: I have seen so much hurtful blogging on the Internet. What if someone just blogged to build one life? What if someone wrote a word of encouragement rather than a tirade of criticism?

Have you ever noticed God never asks what we have done with what we don't have? He has never asked me what I would do with Celine Dion's singing voice. He knows I just don't have it. He is interested in hearing about what I do with what He has entrusted to my care.

A Biblical Example

I fear we are too quick to judge how others steward their gifts and money while we neglect to steward our own well. We each have been given a talent, a God-entrusted portion of ability. And the day will come when each and every one of us will reveal how we stewarded this God portion. He will not be interested in hearing our opinions about how other people have stewarded their portions. He will ask us only what we did with ours.

This is not merely a feel-good-about-yourself life lesson. This is a kingdom of heaven principle. In other words, this is a very big idea to God, so no matter how many times you have read this Scripture, open your heart to review it in perhaps a different light.

Again, the Kingdom of Heaven can be illustrated by the story of a man going on a long trip. He called together his servants and entrusted his money to them while he was gone.

(MATTHEW 25:14)

216

Let's frame this so there is no question: this is Jesus giving each of us, His servants, the mandate to increase His kingdom and multiply His influence on Earth. While He is busy preparing places for us in heaven, we are to be busy on Earth. To accomplish this increase in His absence, there is a distribution of resources.

He gave five bags of silver to one, two bags of silver to another, and one bag of silver to the last—dividing it in proportion to their abilities. He then left on his trip.

(MATTHEW 25:15)

Here is where we find out God thinks differently from the rest of us. In the interest of being "nice," we probably would have somehow devised a way to make it all equal for everyone. We would have painstakingly divided the eight talents into equal portions (each person would have received 2.66 bags of silver) so everyone would feel good about him- or herself and know that God was fair. Let's do the math on this distribution and see what God's return would have been: according to parable calculations, this would have only yielded a return of 13.3 bags of silver!

The truth is God is more than fair . . . God is just. And when abilities are not equal, distribution should not be equal either. After all, would Donald Trump give the most money to the least talented—just to be nice? Of course not. He knows that would be irresponsible. And he labors to build only an earthly kingdom—how much more careful should we be with God's economy? Our perspective is skewed because we are too frequently earthbound. Heaven has a different perspective and economy. God wisely gives according to abilities, not inabilities. Watch what happens.

The truth is God is more than fair . . . God is just.

The servant who received the five bags of silver began to invest the money and earned five more. The servant with two bags of silver also went to work and earned two more. But the servant who received the one bag of silver dug a hole in the ground and hid the master's money. (MATTHEW 25:16–18)

The first two doubled their money and the last one buried his treasure. The total return on the entrusted money was fifteen bags of silver, but it should have been at least sixteen. The two servants who doubled what had been entrusted to them by their master got the same response:

The master was full of praise. "Well done, my good and faithful servant. You have been faithful in handling this small amount, so now I will give you many more responsibilities. Let's celebrate together!" (MATTHEW 25:21, 23)

They were excited to see their master return and he was excited by the return they brought to him and in response he entrusted them with many more responsibilities. Then he decided to throw a party for everyone ... well, not quite everyone was going to be invited. The third servant was not excited, he was actually rather rude when his master returned.

Then the servant with the one bag of silver came and said, "Master, I knew you were a harsh man, harvesting crops you didn't plant and gathering crops you didn't cultivate. I was afraid I would lose your money, so I hid it in the earth. Look, here is your money back." (MATTHEW 25:24–25)

He called his master a "hard man," but the first two servants made no such judgment calls. They spoke only of stew-

218

ardship and return. Then the grumpy one went on to say the master was a bit of a thief, harvesting and gathering what he did not cultivate—another less-than-complimentary remark. Needless to say, the master was not pleased.

> *But the master replied, "You wicked and lazy servant! If you knew I harvested crops I didn't plant and gathered crops I didn't cultivate, why didn't you deposit my money in the bank? At least I could have gotten some interest on it." Then he ordered, "Take the money from this servant, and give it to the one with the ten bags of silver. To those who use well what they are given, even more will be given, and they will have an abundance. But from those who do nothing, even what little they have will be taken away."* (MATTHEW 25:26–29)

Let's check out all the judgments against this third servant. First, he was wicked, which means he twisted things. Second, he was lazy, which means he was a horrible steward of time. Third, he was just plain stupid because he didn't respond appropriately. Just an ordinary Joe would have at least earned interest on the bag of silver rather than merely digging a hole to hide it. And the last charge against him: the master called him unfaithful, which means he could not be trusted. Yikes!

Fear Interferes

How did an entrusted servant go so wrong? I am certain there are more reasons than we have space to explore, but there is one of interest here I would like to note. We find it among the servant's own words: "I was afraid." Do you hear this? I have learned that if people speak long enough, they will give themselves away. This servant was a coward.

Understand that fear will ultimately make you do things you

would never dream of doing, say things you would never dream of saying, listen to things you should never give ear to. Fear will cause you to view things in such a twisted manner that you lose all healthy sense of perspective. Then you will doubt what you should trust and trust what you should doubt. Fear is insidious, and if there was only one thing I could impart to each and every woman today, it would be an empowerment to live fearlessly.

I prayed to the LORD, and he answered me. He freed me from all my fears. Those who look to him for help will be radiant with joy; no shadow of shame will darken their faces.

(PSALM 34:4–5)

God knows what each of us can handle. If five bags of gold had been given to the servant who buried the money, the total return would have been disastrous: only eleven bags of gold.

I have heard so many people say things like "If I had money, I would give it." No, they wouldn't. Because the truth is, we all have more than we know right now. We have just forgotten what we have because it is buried.

Fear will cause you to view things in such a twisted manner that you lose all healthy sense of perspective.

Perhaps you were afraid that if you invested what God gave you, you would lose it. Beautiful one, that is just not true! This is the season of multiplication and God is unearthing the buried talents in His daughters—all for the purpose of and to empower nurture.

Was it not the heart of a princess that sheltered Moses?

Soon Pharaoh's daughter came down to bathe in the river, and her attendants walked along the riverbank. When the

220

*princess saw the basket among the reeds, she sent her maid
to get it for her. When the princess opened it, she saw the
baby. The little boy was crying, and she felt sorry for him.
"This must be one of the Hebrew children," she said. Then
the baby's sister approached the princess. "Should I go and
find one of the Hebrew women to nurse the baby for you?"
she asked.* (EXODUS 2:5–7)

What awoke the compassion of this princess? The helpless cries of an infant. What will awaken your compassion?
The beautiful thing is that the compassion of a princess and
the ingenuity of a sister restored an infant to the nurture of
his mother. But this is not merely an ancient story—even
today many princesses and sisters are making just such dynamic connections as well. Women the world over are responding to the cries of those marked for destruction and
intervening to save and restore life. I've had the amazing opportunity to partner with some effective and compassionate
people.

*God places the lonely in families; he sets the prisoners free
and gives them joy. But he makes the rebellious live in a sun-
scorched land.* (PSALM 68:6)

One such strategic organization took this Scripture as its
blueprint for rescuing orphans in Uganda. The staff knew
the problem was not just a housing issue, but that these
beautiful children had lost all sense of home. When there
is no home, there is no center of nurture to raise up the
next generation of leaders. Without leaders, the country fal-
ters once again and resources are squandered as corruption
abounds.

God is unearthing the buried talents in His daughters—all for the purpose of and to empower nurture.

As I wrote this book, my life crossed the path of Marilyn Skinner, a beautiful, petite Canadian woman who for more than two decades has labored to build homes for the sons and daughters of Uganda. Along with her husband, Gary, Marilyn founded Watoto and just one of the many beautiful things they're doing is putting a widow with eight children into a home of their own. Messenger International has partnered with Watoto to build just such a home.

Perhaps like me you have wondered what you can do as one lone woman. Well, if compassion has enlarged your heart, then it is your time to do something. You can give as an individual or you can gather others to partner with you as you reach out. You could sponsor a child through an organization such as Compassion. You can feed the starving and destitute by partnering with Life Outreach or build a home for orphans by joining with organizations such as Watoto.

I believe in the next decade women are going to rise up and partner with each other to see the destructive reign of poverty come to an end. In the back of the book I have listed information on some of the organizations that are reaching out and touching the lives of the hurting. I would love you to be aware of just a few of the many worthy organizations you could partner with as well.

12

Your Part

PART (noun): An essential portion or integral element.[1]

Albert Einstein wrote, "Everything should be made as simple as possible, but not simpler." The operative word here is *simple*. Understand, *simple* does not always mean *easy*. I know that what I am asking you to do will not be easy, but it will be simple, straightforward, and uncomplicated. Jesus always turned what the religious leaders had complicated and compiled into elaborate lists of do's and don'ts into simplified word pictures that a child could understand. When truth is in its purest, childlike form, the Word becomes flesh.

There are simple yet powerful steps you can use to start yourself down the path of God's beauty, freedom, purpose, and wholeness for your life. Allow God's Word to nurture your dreams and hopes. The Word has the power to create an atmosphere that fosters the right conditions for this to happen, but the time comes when each of us must make our own choices.

As daughters of heaven, will we choose to be powerful or to

remain victims? Will we move forward or stay tethered to what is so long passed? Will we continue to live an isolated existence or will we purposefully connect—and nurture each other? The choices are before us.

Make Your Move

The following points of action are ones only you can initiate. No one can pray you through this process. Yes, someone can pray the conditions would be right, but when all the information is given...it is you who must make your move.

Beautiful one, the hour is late. Some of you are tired, but it is not yet time to sleep. It is time to awake. There are captive daughters in every age bracket and it is time they were free. Most of us have spent far too much time in a position of slavery when we are in fact royalty. We need to unleash the gift of nurture in all captive women and lead them to live in their true inheritance.

> *Most of us have spent far too much time in a position of slavery when we are in fact royalty.*

It is my prayer that hope and the desire for more than an existence have awakened your strength. It is time to couple truth with action. Throughout His walk on Earth, Jesus encountered people who earnestly wanted answers, but when He gave the answers they shut down.

It wasn't because what He asked was too complicated. That was the religious leaders' approach. No, they drew back because what He shared was simple but hard. How complex is "Follow Me," especially when Jesus is standing right in front of you?

Often what He asked was not difficult for the onlookers, but it was a major challenge to that individual in that moment.

As you review the action points, some will be relatively easy for you, but others will be just plain hard—not impossible, but difficult because they will challenge the way you have always functioned.

To simplify the process I am going to set them up as though it was a day—the metaphorical "day" when you choose to change your course. Do not underestimate the power of choice—it is very significant. Even if nothing measurable happens right away, your choice is momentous because it is the beginning.

I distinctly remember the day my life began to change. I would love to say it happened while I was praying for the nations, but actually I was putting on makeup. As I adjusted the mirror, I heard the Holy Spirit drop these words into my spirit: "This day your life changes."

It was so profound and completely unexpected that I just stopped and stared at my reflection. Everything looked the same. What had I done to inspire such a declaration? Understand, I had looked for change. For years I'd cried out for transformation. Why was this suddenly the day?

Now I have my answer. The only thing I'd done differently that morning was to follow through on a decision I'd made months prior. My actions did not seem all that significant. They were steps in the correct direction. I was reaching beyond every major comfort zone I had painstakingly erected. I was moving outside myself into my destiny and knew it not.

Are you ready to step into your destiny?

Step 1: Awake

AWAKE (verb): Meaning to cease to sleep. To excite from a state resembling sleep; as from death, stupidity, or inaction; to put into action, or new life.[2]

Waking is how we naturally begin each day, so it stands to reason we must awake spiritually to this new day as well.

This is all the more urgent, for you know how late it is; time is running out. Wake up, for our salvation is nearer now than when we first believed. The night is almost gone; the day of salvation will soon be here.   (ROMANS 13:11–12)

The period of time we now inhabit is referred to as "the night," which is almost over. It appears we presently wander our earth in its final moments of darkness, preceding the dawn of salvation. Celtic lore called this the "time between times." We are poised on the brink of a new day's dawn and we are to awake and prepare in anticipation of its arrival.

We are poised on the brink of a new day's dawn and we are to awake and prepare.

In God's kingdom we first receive in and through the spirit, then we experience it in the natural realm. For example, salvation was appropriated in the spirit when we were born again, but the day is coming when we will receive salvation on every level.

Scripture compares our waking to righteousness by denying our sin nature to the shedding of up dirty garments and the repentance of evil deeds. The waking process encompasses repentance, which is the process of stripping one's self of darkness.

Once awake, we must move to our next step because it does us no good to remain in bed.

Step 2: Arise

ARISE (verb): 1. To rise from a quiet, inactive, or subjugated state to become active or vocal. To move upward to a higher place or level. To stand up from sitting, lying, or kneeling.[3]

Once awake, we need to arise. If we don't, we run the risk of falling back asleep. I have placed my alarm clock across the room. When it goes off, I have to rise to turn it off. Before implementing this I used to hit the snooze button and return to sleep without a conscious awareness of what I'd done.

We are called to something contrary to our nature, our comfort, and the dark surroundings we occupy; we are called to light.

It is human nature to want to sleep when it is dark, but we are called to something contrary to our nature, our comfort, and the dark surroundings we occupy; we are called to light.

Awake, O sleeper, rise up from the dead, and Christ will give you light. (EPHESIANS 5:14)

When we arise, we change our position. God awakens us so we can rise above what has been and move into what will be. Once awake we put off the old and move onto the new. Yesterday and its deeds are dead and gone.

The day the Spirit told me my life was going to change I was awake but I had not risen. I still walked in guilt, shame, and condemnation. Each night I searched my day and reviewed my actions in light of the darkness. I had a list of infractions that left me so overwhelmed I usually resorted to justifying my actions and choices. I awoke each morning to darkness rather than to light. I felt burdened—I wanted to shed my "evil deeds" of yesterday but did not know how.

Once the darkness is dealt with, Christ gives us light. After we are up, we are to proceed to the next step.

Step 3: Attire

ATTIRE (verb): To dress yourself or somebody else, especially in clothes of a particular type.[4]

So remove your dark deeds like dirty clothes, and put on the shining armor of right living. (ROMANS 13:12)

To dress, you normally have to undress. Take off night wear, put on light. Once sin is confessed, consider it removed. We then attire ourselves in light. This means we exchange a sin-darkness-unbelief consciousness for a faith-light-belief consciousness.

Do you know why I remained in the darkness for so long after being born again? I was captive to unbelief. This leads to our next step.

Step 4: Aware

AWARE (adjective): To be mindful that something exists because you notice it or realize that it is happening.[5]

We must live in the Spirit with an awareness of God. He is good. He is willing. He is present. He is love. He is holy. He is faithful. He is true. He is the great I AM, both beginning and end.

You see, I believed that *God was* but forgot that *He is.* I doubted Him in the present and screened Him through my past. I doubted that He would in fact answer my prayers. Why? It wasn't that I thought He was unable—that might have been bearable. No, I imagined He was unwilling. I never felt good or disciplined enough to merit His attention or favor. My soul became aware when I began to believe.

I believed that **God** was *but forgot that* **He** is.

When you truly get the revelation of His goodness, mercy, and love, you can't help but live in a constant and ever-increasing awareness of His love, light, and beauty. You begin to move through life differently, which sets us up for the next step.

Step 5: Attitude

ATTITUDE (noun): A physical posture, either conscious or unconscious, especially while interacting with others.[6]

Wake up, my heart! Wake up, O lyre and harp! I will wake the dawn with my song. (PSALM 57:8)

You have the opportunity to set your attitude first thing in the morning. Rather than waiting for life to happen to you, hasten toward life by laying hold of your attitude. David had a song that set his day in motion. Have you ever heard a song when you woke up? Begin to sing it. The song within David roused his soul to both worship God and seize his day.

As for me, I will see Your face in righteousness; I shall be satisfied when I awake in Your likeness. (PSALM 17:15 NKJV)

Listen to his attitude. There is absolutely no doubt that God is righteous and that David is in the process of transformation into God's likeness. Just like David, you are being transformed daily and renewed from the inside out. The day will come when this is revealed in all its fullness, but until then we have to develop the right attitude.

> ### *The world is not happening to us—we are happening to it.*

The world is not happening to us—we are happening to it. The light is far more powerful than the darkness and it is time we acted as if this was true. We need to lose the Christian escape-the-world mentality and be those who overcome in this world.

> No, *despite all these things, overwhelming victory is ours through Christ, who loved us. And I am convinced that nothing can ever separate us from God's love. Neither death nor life, neither angels nor demons, neither our fears for today nor our worries about tomorrow—not even the powers of hell can separate us from God's love. No power in the sky above or in the earth below—indeed, nothing in all creation will ever be able to separate us from the love of God that is revealed in Christ Jesus our Lord.* (ROMANS 8:37–39)

This declaration leaves no margin for error! As He is, so we are... which brings us to our next step.

Step 6: Asset

ASSET (noun): Somebody or something that is useful and contributes to the success of something.[7]

You are a vital part of this victory. Inside you are both worthy and necessary contributions. You are an asset to this world.

You, beautiful one, are an answer, not a problem. Actually, daughter, you are a part of the solution to the human crisis. There is a gift deep within only you can give. You must find this strength, this talent, this ability and give it to others. God has hidden an asset within your soul.

> **Daughter, you are a part of the solution to the human crisis.**

Please understand, I know that God alone is the ultimate answer and source of our strength.

I love you, Lord; you are my strength.   (Psalm 18:1)

But this revelation does not negate our God-given attributes and assets. There is a beautiful interdependence played out when we love Him with all our might and He becomes our source of strength, and within the shelter of His wings we discover our might.

Step 7: Approach

Approach (verb): To move closer to somebody or something.

There is no quicker way to move closer to God than to declare who and where He is.

There was a time when my world was rocked. I felt shaky and disoriented. Every safe boundary I'd known had been breached. What I had thought to be true proved to be false. If my strength had been found in people, I could not have stood. In the midst of all this, I lay down to take a nap one day to clear the fog in my brain. I rested for about twenty minutes and woke suddenly when my dog jumped off the bed.

Before my thoughts could engage I heard my spirit declaring the might of God. I listened to what was being rehearsed in my head. Suddenly I realized I needed to speak aloud what I was hearing within. I declared the might of God, and almost instantly all the troubles were dwarfed by the awesomeness of the Most High God. The weights that had attached themselves fell away as I approached His throne.

This High Priest of ours understands our weaknesses, for he faced all of the same testings we do, yet he did not sin. So let us come boldly to the throne of our gracious God. There we will receive his mercy, and we will find grace to help us when we need it most. (HEBREWS 4:15–16)

When I approach His throne, I acknowledge His supremacy. When I approach Him I come boldly, not timidly, afraid, and unbelieving. And once I am there I...

Step 8: Ask

ASK (verb): To put a question to somebody. To make a request for something.

Far too many daughters are afraid to ask for what they need. Let me rephrase that a bit: too many women ask the wrong person for what they need. God wants us to feel free to come to Him. Remember one of the qualities of daughters? Healthy daughters ask questions. Healthy daughters are not afraid to ask for what they need. When my children are ill, I know they are feeling better when they ask for food and drink. It is time we asked for what we need to recover our strength.

Healthy daughters are not afraid to ask for what they need.

God invites us to ask. Actually He urges us repeatedly to ask Him for whatever we need. I fear you might doubt your grounds or right to ask, so let's look deeper.

I found a powerful example of sisters who were united and persuasive as they asked God for what appeared to be denied the daughters. Here is the record of these five daughters who made a request and fostered change and altered the course of legacy.

One day a petition was presented by the daughters of Zelo-phehad—Mahlah, Noah, Hoglah, Milcah, and Tirzah. Their father, Zelophehad, was a descendant of Hepher son of Gilead, son of Makir, son of Manasseh, son of Joseph. These women stood before Moses, Eleazar the priest, the tribal leaders, and the entire community at the entrance of the Tabernacle. "Our father died in the wilderness," they said. "He was not among Korah's followers, who rebelled against the LORD*; he died because of his own sin. But he had no sons. Why should the name of our father disappear from his clan just because he had no sons? Give us property along with the rest of our relatives."* (NUMBERS 27:1–4)

This was a pretty gutsy move. Do you remember what was going on back then? The earth had been known to open up and swallow people! The Israelites had just finished a forty-year time-out in the desert where a lot of people had perished. A new season was beginning and allotments of the promised land were being portioned and assigned.

In this climate, five daughters showed up and questioned how leadership was appropriating the land. The rule, which was and always had been, was the inheritance passed down through the sons...not the daughters. The parceling of the promised land would be no different.

These sisters could have gathered together and complained and cried among themselves about how unfair God and His laws were. They also could have just accepted their circumstances and hoped perhaps to marry into some land. Instead, they thought through the situation and acted wisely. They agreed on a strategy, constructed a petition, and approached the tabernacle. These daughters stood as one before Moses, the high priest, leaders, and the whole assembly and made their case.

No one had ever raised the question of what would happen if a family had no sons. No one had thought to address this issue, so there was no precedent from which Moses could make a judgment. He was unsure how to answer, so Moses did what any godly man should do: he went to God.

So Moses brought their case before the LORD. And the LORD replied to Moses, "The claim of the daughters of Zelophehad is legitimate. You must give them a grant of land along with their father's relatives. Assign them the property that would have been given to their father. And give the following instructions to the people of Israel: If a man dies and has no son, then give his inheritance to his daughters."

(NUMBERS 27:5–8)

Wow, imagine how these five daughters must have felt! The God of heaven and Earth declared their claim to both land and promise legitimate. God did not just rule on their behalf, He created a statute for all of Israel. This was actually the last ruling Moses made before he left this earth. As God's people entered into their season of promise, inheritance would be passed down to daughters whenever there was no son to carry the father's name. How amazing!

This Old Testament interaction makes me wonder how often we just accept things God would welcome us to question.

These daughters did what they were born to do. Their personal quest eventually encompassed so much more than their family claim. Their respectful, constructive challenge of status quo brought a different perspective to the assembly of male leadership. Inheritance would have been lost to thousands of families without their intercession and input.

I hear this entreaty from heaven:
"Ask, daughters, ask!"

In my spirit I hear this entreaty from heaven: "Ask, daughters, ask!" It is heaven's voice asking to be revealed on Earth. The goodness of God invites all to taste and see that He is in fact good.

> *Your Father knows exactly what you need even before you*
> *ask him!* (MATTHEW 6:8)

Jesus is excited about sharing this—notice the exclamation point! Do not imagine for a second that the Father was surprised or caught off guard by the request of these sisters. Moses and the assembled leaders might have been, but not God.

> *For everyone who asks, receives. Everyone who seeks, finds.*
> *And to everyone who knocks, the door will be opened.*
> (MATTHEW 7:8)

In my opinion, the most poignant invitation to ask transpired between Jesus and the Samaritan woman. Jesus was alone at a well when a woman approached to draw water.

> *Please give me a drink.* (JOHN 4:7)

He politely asked water of a Samaritan woman with a questionable reputation. The woman was surprised. What was a Jewish male doing talking to a Samaritan female? And what was He thinking, asking her to handle His water? She wondered if there was something more to what He was asking. Before answering, she asked a question of Him:

> The woman was surprised, for Jews refuse to have anything to do with Samaritans. She said to Jesus, "You are a Jew, and I am a Samaritan woman. Why are you asking me for a drink?" Jesus replied, "If you only knew the gift God has for you and who you are speaking to, you would ask me, and I would give you living water." (JOHN 4:9–10)

Do you hear what Jesus said to this Samaritan woman? If you missed it, hear it now, beautiful daughter. He is challenging all of us: "If *you* only knew." In this verse He is inviting us to expand the way we look at everything. His words are reaching out through this woman to us: "If *you* only knew the gift God has for *you* and who *you* are speaking to, *you* would ask me."

Daughter, you were born to entreat heaven.

In this encounter Jesus specifically invited a daughter, a woman, to ask Him for something. He invited her to ask for the gift God had for her—living water. Daughter, you were born to entreat heaven.

> I tell you the truth, anyone who believes in me will do the same works I have done, and even greater works, because I am going to be with the Father. You can ask for anything in my name, and I will do it, so that the Son can bring glory to the Father. Yes, ask me for anything in my name, and I will do it! (JOHN 14:12–14)

There is no gender, race, or age disqualification here, just an invitation for anyone to ask in His name. Daughter, sister, mother, friend, I fear we ask too little because we think too small. Perhaps we have felt isolated, inconsequential, weak, feminine, and inadequate, but nothing is farther from the truth. You are powerful and your questions are essential. What you would ask for the world has need of. The Son brings glory to the Father when He answers what we ask.

The sons of Earth have been empowered to ask and that is good and well. They should ask. But the time has come when the daughters must join their voices with the sons'. You see, daughters ask for very different things from what sons ask for. Do you remember what I said earlier—men plan wars, but women plan weddings? When you are preparing for a wedding, you ask for very different items than you do when you are preparing for war. Both are on the horizon and it is our time to ask.

In this encounter with Jesus, our beautiful friend the Samaritan woman asked about so many things: worship, prejudice, living water, relationships, the prophetic, the Messiah. And when she had her answers, she ran and invited others to come and see as well.

Perhaps you are afraid to ask for fear you'll be disappointed. Maybe you are afraid you will ask for the wrong things. Or do you fear that you might ask for the wrong reasons? Jesus settled this issue for us.

And I will ask the Father, and he will give you another Advocate, who will never leave you. He is the Holy Spirit, who leads into all truth. The world cannot receive him, because it isn't looking for him and doesn't recognize him. But you know him, because he lives with you now and later will be in you.

(JOHN 14:16–17)

And again:

But if you remain in me and my words remain in you, you may ask for anything you want, and it will be granted! When you produce much fruit, you are my true disciples. This brings great glory to my Father. (JOHN 15:7–8)

We have the promise of the Holy Spirit to lead us. His words will rightly divide our motives and when we ask anything birthed in this dynamic, it will be granted or arranged.

Why should we ask? Why not just allow what is going to happen to happen? Because "true disciples produce much fruit," and you can't bear fruit without asking. Why do we want to be fruitful? Is it so we can feel validated as women? No, it is the way we glorify our Father. I almost wish I could plead with you in person and add voice to my words. Beautiful daughters, ask!

There is something this world needs that only you know how to ask for. You are the one to see the situation and entreat heaven. Remember Zechariah's prayer? He thought he was asking only for a son, when really it was an answer for a nation!

When you see a need, ask God for the answer. When you see injustice, ask Him to execute justice. If you are alone, ask Him to show you how to be a companion. Ask for beauty. Ask for laughter. Ask for safety. Ask for equality of the sexes. Ask for the power of the Spirit. Ask for a mother. Ask for a daughter. Ask for a grandmother. Ask for the provision you need. Ask to be a friend. Ask for seed to sow. Ask for bread to eat. Ask for the power to forgive.

The list is endless and the need is urgent. Once you have asked, then it is time to . . .

Step 9: Act

ACT (verb): The action of carrying something out.

There is nothing left but to *do*. You are writing one aspect of heaven's involvement on Earth each and every day. There were gospels and letters to churches, but the story we are a part of is yet to be completed: we are the modern-day book of Acts. The story is not over and the race is not complete—we are part of an enormous relay! There are batons to be transported and eventually handed off. The runners match speed for the hand-off, then one slows while the other takes off. Perhaps this is the reason it is called the human race.

Therefore, since we are surrounded by such a huge crowd of witnesses to the life of faith, let us strip off every weight that slows us down, especially the sin that so easily trips us up. And let us run with endurance the race God has set before us. (HEBREWS 12:1)

Run well, daughter.
You are watched for, loved, and well able.

You are writing one aspect of heaven's involvement on Earth each and every day.

Putting It to Practice

Watoto

www.watoto.com
1-866-492-8686

Watoto accomplishes its mission of raising Ugandan leaders by focusing on the essential needs of parentless children—specifically the physical, educational, emotional, and spiritual needs. Founded in 1992, Watoto takes in orphaned children between the ages of two and twelve and places them in families, providing food, shelter, education, health care, and family values. Watoto currently operates three children's villages and cares for over fifteen hundred children. It also contains a complete school system for the Watoto children and the surrounding communities, a medical clinic, a church/community center, an agricultural project providing food, a clean water source, and electrical power. The result is self-sustaining villages that serve the children while providing employment for women and teachers, and steady jobs for laborers.

LIFE Outreach International

www.lifetoday.org
1-800-947-LIFE (5433)
In Australia: 1-800-99-9901
In Europe: 0800-043-5361

LIFE Outreach International is an organization committed to the commission of Jesus Christ to take the gospel to all nations. LIFE believes that Christ intended for us to demonstrate His love as well as proclaim it. LIFE has several ministries worldwide that are actively demonstrating the love of God. These ministries include Mission Feeding, Water for LIFE, *LIFE TODAY* television, evangelistic campaigns, and LIFE Care Centers for children. Millions of hurting, desperate people all over the world have experienced the compassion and provision of Jesus Christ through various humanitarian relief programs sponsored by LIFE Outreach International.

Compassion International

www.compassion.com
1-800-336-7676

Compassion International is a Christian child development organization dedicated to releasing children from poverty. Their ministry is twofold: They work through local churches to provide child development programs to deliver children from economic, physical, social, and spiritual poverty, enabling them to become responsible, fulfilled Christian adults. They also speak out for children in poverty, informing, motivating, and equipping others to become advocates for children.

Hillsong Colour Sisterhood

www2.hillsong.com/sisterhood
+61-2-8853-5353

The Colour Sisterhood is an amazing organization representing a company of down-to-earth, everyday women who desire to make a difference and make their world a better place. In essence, it is a foundation that exists to place value upon humanity. The Colour Sisterhood champions the cause of the orphan child and widow, comes alongside women near and far who face challenges, and it ultimately seeks to influence nations with the goodness and answers that are to be found in God. The Colour Sisterhood is about empowering you to become the helper God created you to be. Women are created with ears that often hear the cry before others, hearts that respond quickly, and arms that are always willing—they want to put tools in your hand, provide some God-inspiration, and cheer you along the way!

Notes

Chapter 1

1. *Encarta® World English Dictionary* [North American Edition] © & (P)2004 Microsoft Corporation. All rights reserved. Developed for Microsoft by Bloomsbury Publishing Plc.(Included in Microsoft Word 2004 software.) Some of the definitions I use in this book are abbreviated forms from the *Encarta Dictionary*.
2. P. D. Eastman, *Are You My Mother?* (New York: Random House Books for Young Readers, 1960.)

Chapter 2

1. *Encarta World English Dictionary.*
2. Marianne Williamson, *A Return to Love* (New York: HarperCollins, 1992); http://marianne.com/book/index.htm. Note: My use of this quote, which I believe will strengthen and encourage my readers, should not imply that I necessarily endorse all of Marianne's teachings or ideas.

Chapter 3

1. http://www.answers.com/topic/mother?cat=health
2. *Encarta World English Dictionary.*
3. Ibid.
4. Abbreviated definition from: http://encarta.msn.com/dictionary_/relate.html

Chapter 4

1. *Encarta World English Dictionary.*
2. *Noah Webster's First Edition of an American Dictionary of the English Language* (San Francisco: Foundation for American Christian Education, 1967, 1995), 72.
3. *Encarta World English Dictionary.*
4. Ibid.
5. Abbreviated definition from: http://encarta.msn.com/dictionary_/gossip.html.
6. Editors of the American Heritage Dictionary, *Roget's II: The New Thesaurus*, 3rd ed. (New York: Houghton Mifflin Company, 1995.) http://www.answers.com/isolation?cat=health

Chapter 5

1. http://www.answers.com/true?cat=technology
2. *Noah Webster's.*
3. *Encarta World English Dictionary.*

Chapter 6

1. *Encarta World English Dictionary.*
2. *Noah Webster's,* 113.
3. http://net.bible.org/dictionary.php?word=Conscience
4. http://net.bible.org/home.php
5. http://net.bible.org/dictionary.php?word=Hearthttp://net.bible.org/dictionary.php?word=Heart
6. *Noah Webster's,* 87.

Chapter 7

1. *American Heritage Dictionary.*
2. *Holman Illustrated Bible Dictionary* (Nashville, TN: Holman Reference, 2003), 1174.
3. *Strong's Greek Concordance,* www.htmlbible.com/sacrednamebible com/kjvstrongs/STRINDEX.htm

Chapter 8

1. *Encarta World English Dictionary.*
2. Brown, Driver, Briggs, and Gesenius, "Hebrew Lexicon entry for Gabar," *The KJV Old Testament Hebrew Lexicon*: http://www.biblestu dytools.net/Lexicons/Hebrew/heb.cgi?number=1396&version=kjv
3. http://www.babynamenetwork.com/baby_names/detail.cfm?name=Elizabeth&gender=Female

4. From Matthew Henry: "Her name was Mary, the same name with Miriam, the sister of Moses and Aaron; the name signifies exalted, and a great elevation it was to her indeed to be thus favoured above all the daughters of the house of David." Note on Luke 1:26–38 from *Matthew Henry's Commentary on the Whole Bible: New Modern Edition*, Electronic Database (Hendrickson Publishers Inc., 1991). From behindthenames.com: "Usual English form of *Maria*, which was the Latin form of the New Testament Greek names Μαριαμ *(Mariam)* or Μαρια *(Maria)* (the spellings are interchangeable), which were from the Hebrew name מרים *(Miryam)*. The meaning is not known for certain, but there are several theories including 'sea of bitterness,' 'rebelliousness,' and 'wished for child.' However it was most likely originally an Egyptian name, perhaps derived in part from *mry* 'beloved' or *mr* 'love.'"

Chapter 9
1. *Encarta World English Dictionary.*
2. Ibid.

Chapter 10
1. *Encarta World English Dictionary.*
2. http://encarta.msn.com/dictionary_1861585040/ambassador.html

Chapter 11
1. *Encarta World English Dictionary.*

Chapter 12
1. *Encarta World English Dictionary.*
2. Ibid.
3. Ibid.
4. Ibid.
5. Ibid.
6. Ibid.
7. Ibid.

nurture

Give and Get What You Need to Flourish

**Contact Messenger International
for more information on the
Nurture Curriculum**

Fight Like *a Girl*
The Power of Being a Woman

You are an answer, not a problem.

Curriculum Includes

*12 - 30 Minute Sessions on 4 DVDs
Hardback Book and Interactive Workbook
Makeup Bag
Bracelet - Genuine Swarovski Austrian Crystal
Advertising Poster and Bookmark*

In *Fight Like a Girl*, Lisa challenges the status quo that women need to fit into the role of a man, and she leads you in the truth of what it means to be a woman. Discover how to express your God-given strengths and fulfill your role in the community, workplace, home, and church. This curriculum will encourage you to find your true potential and realize you are an answer and not a problem.

KISSED GIRLS AND MADE THEM CRY

Kit Includes

*4 Sessions on 2 DVDs
Bonus Q&A
Best-Selling Book
Interactive Workbook
Advertising Poster*

Don't believe the lie—sexual purity isn't about rules...it's about freedom and power. It is time to take back what we've cheaply given away. This kit is for women of all ages who long for a greater intimacy with Jesus and need to embrace God's healing and restoring love.

*"I'm 15, and through your kit my nightmare has been
turned back to a dream!"*

Books by Lisa

Be Angry, But Don't Blow It!
Fight Like a Girl
Kissed the Girls and Made Them Cry
Nurture
Out of Control and Loving It!
The True Measure of a Woman
You Are Not What You Weigh

WOMEN:
Sign up to receive
EMAILS from Lisa!

Visit us online at: www.MessengerInternational.org

Messenger
International.
life-transforming truth.

For more information
please contact us:

UNITED STATES	EUROPE	AUSTRALIA
PO Box 888	PO Box 622	PO Box 6200
Palmer Lake, CO	Newport, NP19 8ZJ	Dural, D.C. NSW 2158
80133-0888	UNITED KINGDOM	AUSTRALIA
800-648-1477 (US & Canada)	**Tel: 44 (0) 870-745-5790**	In AUS 1-300-650-577
Tel: 719-487-3000	Fax: 44 (0) 870-745-5791	**Tel: +61 2 8850 1725**
Fax: 719-487-3300	europe@MessengerInternational.org	Fax +61 2 8850 1735
mail@MessengerInternational.org		australia@MessengerInternational.org

www.MessengerInternational.org